INTEGRATING PLAY THERAPY AND EMDR WITH CHILDREN

Victoria McGuinness

A Guide for Parents - Can be copied and used to give to parents to help explain experiential play therapy

Using EMDR and Play Therapy With Your Child - Can be copied and used to give to parents to help explain EMDR.

Parent's Guide for Family Play Therapy Sessions - "Things are different in here!" - Can be copied and used to give to parents before a family play session.

STAGES OF PLAY THERAPY GRAPH (Norton's Model: Reprinted with the author's permission). Protected under the original copyright. Not to be reproduced.

1stBooks-rev 02/18/03

TABLE OF CONTENTS

INTRODUCTION

This handbook is not intended to be training in EMDR, per se, although many uses of EMDR with children are addressed. Primarily, this workbook is intended to provide training in the use of traditional child-centered, experiential play therapy with children. Weaving the play therapy and EMDR together as treatment methods, when appropriate, is the focus of this handbook for practitioners.

This material is designed for treating children aged toddler through twelve, or post-language through twelve. Formal training in BOTH EMDR and PLAY/CHILD therapy is assumed to have been obtained prior to using the techniques in this book and/or working with young children with these modalities.

The content of this workbook is copyrighted. The inclusion of any other person's material has been credited to that person or organization. This workbook is a summary of a workshop with the same title. The workshop is approved for 6.0 CEU'S toward RPT (Registered Play Therapist) certification through the APT. (Association for Play Therapy, Inc.) Reading this workbook does not provide any continuing education hours toward RPT. Please direct any inquiries to:

A CHILDREN'S THERAPY PLACE, P.C.
Victoria McGuinness, Director
3009 West Colorado Avenue, Suite "D"
Colorado Springs, CO. 80904
Phone: (719) 386-0870
Fax: (719) 386-0872
e-mail:vicmcplay@akidstherapyplace.com
www.akidstherapyplace.com

This workbook is a summary of the workshop (same title) and my training in play therapy and EMDR as experienced in my playroom. I hope it assists you in integrating EMDR with Play Therapy techniques.

Sincerely,

Victoria McGuinness, November 1997

SECTION 1: Comparing Play Therapy & EMDR: Similarities and Differences in Philosophy and Action

SIMILARITIES
High need for safety
Need to go slow/at the child's pace
Need for parental support
Very Powerful
Use of metaphors & associations
Works from feelings to thoughts
Can elicit spontaneous insights
Indicative of dissociative disorders
Not recommended for psychotic or
schizophrenic children
Use of all available sensory data
Work to protect the child's ego
Respect the child/use toys or symbols
Both use "child-friendly," therapeutic
responses
Brings the unconscious to the surface
Both are extremely effective
Similar goals of adaptive resolution
Can produce increased disturbance
between sessions/parents as co-
therapist(s)
Need for close parent (adult) contact
Need for closure in sessions
Results can be behaviorally measured
and are strongly affected by ongoing
trauma or difficulties.
Good for Big "T" and little "t" trauma
Focus on the experience of the child
and its effects -(Not how it may appear
to others: Big T/Little t.)
Emphasis on early childhood
development

DIFFERENCES
EMDR is more "surgical"
EMDR involves more of the
therapist's agenda
EMDR can be faster
PLAY is child directed
PLAY messages may be more diffuse
PLAY is a more "whole bodied" or
reactive experience of trauma or
tendencies
EMDR uses questions & answers
PLAY uses more statements
PLAY seems more natural; is more
"fun."
The Playroom motivates children to
engage in therapy, it takes more work
to motivate children to use EMDR
PLAY accommodates shorter attention
spans more easily
-Full body integration
-Experiential learning and
reinforcement
-Allows for dramatic life rehearsal
-Natural learning style

The philosophies and actions utilized in both play therapy and EMDR are both polarized to some extent and yet, are extremely complimentary. EMDR can fill in the gaps of play- based therapy or go deeper into issues in a more conscious way. Play can provide rich symbols and material for target selection, SUDS and VoC measurements with children using EMDR. Experiential play therapy also provides the large motor activity and a virtual "theatre" for playing-out or dramatization of the child's story, enabling full body integration of the positive changes that EMDR may produce.

Caution and creativity are the keys to integrating PLAY and EMDR with children. Caution is called for because of the areas in which play therapy and EMDR are most polarized - experiential play therapy is mostly child directed and EMDR is mostly clinician directed. For example, experiential play therapy is almost being totally "child-centered," spontaneous play versus the "questions & answers," involved with EMDR that are directed by the therapist. Further differences include sitting vs. moving, "working," versus "playing," ego protection through play themes vs. direct contact with issues or painful memories. The clinician's ability to keep the relationship SAFE is always essential.

The clinician does not have to warn a child that their play may become very intensive and bring up traumatic experiences. In fact, an entire course of play therapy may occur without ever directly talking about the child's real life experiences especially when the trauma occurred in a pre-verbal stage. But a child needs to be warned or made aware of the potential discomfort(s) that can arise while processing the same trauma using EMDR. When not handled correctly, the child can *and will* feel betrayed by the therapist ESPECIALLY when combined within the play relationship because then the relationship takes on a dual nature. One in which the child is in control and another where the child gives up a lot of the control over issues. However, when EMDR and Play are thoughtfully and sensitively integrated, the results can be remarkable. In fact, the combination of these two very powerful therapies produce beneficial results which far outweigh the potential hazards which can and should be avoided by skilled clinicians.

Often when working with children, outside influences exert pressure for "answers." The parents may need their child to "behave better" to lower their stress, the "X" may or may not approve of therapy, especially "Play therapy and that new fad...EMDR." More often than not, children are currently expelled from school, even pre-school because of aggressive acting-out behaviors and this situation obviously places a lot of stress on the parents, the child and the therapist to find solutions for the child.

Guardian attorneys may want to know who abused the child or they want to protect their adult clients who are accused or suspected of harming a child. Managed care companies often require time-limited treatment plans and may or may not "approve" of EMDR techniques. The rule of thumb is DO NOT RUSH THE CHILD UNDER PRESSURE/DO NOT ABANDON YOUR PLAN (THE CHILD'S PLAY) WHEN PUSHED FOR ANSWERS AND QUICK-FIXES. Maintaining the integrity of the play relationship takes priority over *everything (and everyone) else.* This is easier said than done and it requires a refocused commitment to provide a safe place for the child. In some cases, your playroom or office may be the safest place a child has to be in. Considering the needs of the child over your own need to be politically correct or concern over referrals can be a true act of courage.

In fact, it is much better to leave the parenting time visitation scheduling arrangements, interviewing of the child and other "fact" gathering information to other professionals. Provide immunity from these outside intrusions and pressures on the therapeutic relationship with the child in every possible way. Often, the courts will allow this preservation of the healing relationship for the sake of the child, especially if you, as the child's advocate, stand your ground. Remember, you are the child's voice in the adult world. I have found that when it comes to court proceedings it is best to state and maintain your role as therapist clearly and firmly.

Written reports on the child's progress in therapy are best limited to just that - the child's progress in therapy. Unless there is absolute evidence that can convict a person of child abuse - the best way to serve a child is remain in your role and report the child's experience through your best therapist eyes and the child's heartfelt work with you.

Bear in mind, however, that your input to other professionals involved in a particular case is often very helpful to the child - each interaction needs to be decided on a case-to-case basis. Also bear in mind that you can be made to feel almost as helpless as the children if you cannot fairly execute the role of "expert witness." An "expert witness" is a neutral observer of the facts interpreted through the lens of years of education and experience in the field of mental health. Neutrality is the key to court testimony. If you are a good story teller, organized, prepared and articulate - your testimony in court can accurately bear witness to a child's play themes and messages. Your presence, in behalf of the child, ushers the child's heart, mind and soul to the witness stand that without your testimony, is unoccupied. Stepping outside of your role as therapist can and will harm your testimony and the child's chances for a successful resolution to their case in court.

THERAPEUTIC STAGES IN PLAY THERAPY

**INTEGRATING PLAY THERAPY AND EMDR WITH CHILDREN

Improvement →

Exploratory Stage | Testing for Protection | Dependency Stage | Therapeutic Growth Stage | Termination Stage

B

Install "Safe Place"

Install Positive Beliefs

Look for Themes & Targets

C

Work with NC's
Develop Themes & Targets

Anchor with Safe Place

D

Install

positive growth experiences

& positive beliefs about self

E

friends saying good-bye

Process

Level of Presenting Problem

Time →

Establishment of Trust | Expression of Needs | Empowerment and Closure | Separation

**© V. McGuinness, 6/97.

© 1995 All Rights Reserved
Dr. Byron Norton and Dr. Carol Norton
Family Psychological Services, P.C.
1750 25th Ave., Suite 200

5

SECTION 2: Using EMDR with Children: How is it different from treating adults?

A). General Considerations for letting go of the Adult Protocol

1). The clinician works harder to develop target selection and to develop themes.

2). The clinician works harder and more creatively to engage or motivate a child for treatment, especially an older child who does not want to be in therapy.

3). The process is much more concrete with children than with adults.

4). EMDR may be more imagery-based; associative connections made by the child are less likely; you may have to help make the associations.

5). There is less focus on articulation of cognition, emotions and/or sensations.

6). External objects can be used to elicit motivation, sensations and emotions.

7). Body sensations, pictures and visualizations make the processing easiest.

8). The use of hand-taps, knee-taps, sounds, toys are usually introduced as alternatives to eye movements.

9). Projective techniques with puppets, dolls or stuffed animals used to protect the child's ego need to be readily available.

10). Some children choose to control their own eye-movements (EM), with an object of their choice; shorter sets of EM generally are sufficient for kids.

11). Steps may be omitted or shortened and usually are with the younger ones; shorter sessions focused on EMDR are normal.

12). Children can process very, very quickly; children have shorter channels.

13). Children are less likely to experience abreaction; in fact, oftentimes, it seems like not much is happening (until later) (children are often slow reactors) - it is important to mark changes between sessions.

14). Important to keep the process moving.

15). Can go in and out of play and/or incorporate elements of play.

16). SUDS are very hard to guess in terms of numbers - be creative and get a SUDS level. Simple hand gestures work well… is it little, medium or big? Start with low SUDS to begin unless directed otherwise by the child.

17). Less resolution possible with ongoing disturbances - EMDR may best be postponed if child lives in an emotionally non supportive or destructive environment.

18). Two-handed approach for young children unable to "cross the midline."

19). ADHD kids might want distance from the therapist: two spots on wall, Dr. Shapiro suggests, colored circles, cartoon figures or comic book heroes, etc.

20). Children like being directed to "blow up" or "explode" the picture. (Shapiro, p. 279)

21). Draw problem; draw problem solved (or "all better"). ("Therapeutic Metaphors for Children & the Child Within," 1986 Dr. Joyce Mills and Richard Crowley, Brunner/Mazel, Inc.)

22). Older children will draw and re-draw the "picture" to indicate lowering or increasing SUDS levels as well as helping to measure VoC.

When I feel that integrating EMDR with experiential play therapy would be beneficial to the child, I often start by saying. Will you play a new and different game with me that will help your nightmares to go away? or I wonder where your Safe Place would be and what it would be like, let's try it to see what it would be like to feel calmer or happier, ok?

If I sense some resistance but not an outright "NO!" I remind the child that it will only take a few minutes to try something new.

SECTION 3: Treating Traumatized Children with EMDR & Experiential Play Therapy:

The following excerpt is taken from the work of Dr. Tinker, footnoted (Brier, 1992). I found it so profound that this information is considered news that I've copied here:

> 1). The majority of adults raised in North America, regardless of gender, age, race, ethnicity, or social class, probably experienced some level of maltreatment as children.

> 2). Such negative experiences according to their severity and their interaction with other important variables such as social and familial support, external stressors, and developmental level at the time of maltreatment, can have significant impact on later self-perception, behavior and psychological symptoms.

> 3). Despite the above, the connection between child maltreatment and later dysfunctional or "pathological" behavior has often been overlooked and/or trivialized, partially as a result of cultural acceptance of physical violence, aggression and exploitation in the training and control of children.

A. COMMOM CHARACTERISTICS OF THE TRAUMATIZED CHILD:

Toddlers:

Regression, withdrawal, apathy, anger. Escalate negative behaviors/Increased symptoms of withdrawal.

Three to Five:

Regression (chronic) constipation, diarrhea, loss of mastery of previously learned tasks, separation anxiety, feeling "stuck," issues around saying "no," sadness, depression, fear, intense or frequent nightmares, developmental delays, anger, seemingly inappropriate rage, lack of cooperation, doesn't know when "enough is enough," poor limits, over controlling behaviors, under controlling behaviors, sense of failure, lack of trust and initiative, denial of family problems, difficulty making transitions, wetting, soiling, repetitive behaviors (repetitive/circular play), aggressive treatment of friends or pets, clinging behaviors and over-dependency.

Six to Eight:

Over adapting , school and attention problems, social problems, depression, verbalization of anger, acting out aggression, fears centered on security, self-blame, self-hatred, low self-esteem, victim of parent alienation, victim of divorce (all ages), lying, stealing, being mean to animals and smaller children, inhibited psychological or emotional development, preoccupation with parental issues, boundary problems, eating disorders, hoarding, compulsive behaviors.

Eight to Twelve:

School problems, smoking, drinking, drugging, attention and motivational problems, rejecting compliments, inability to identify needs, withdrawal or escalation, denial of needs, anger, nail biting, starving, bulima, undue procrastination, mistrust of self, feelings and others....trusting the "wrong" people, great ability to COPE.... lying, stealing, depression, lonliness, shame, confusion, lack of spontaneity, lack of creativity, lack of curiosity, lots of unresolvable fears, pain.

ANY AGE: Avoidance &Physiological Hyper-reactivity:

Re-enactment in play, art, behaviors, relationships, being withdrawn, too much day-dreaming/dissociation, avoiding other children, anxiety, sleep and eating disorders, impulsivity, nightmares, etc._ (See Section 11 on Dissociative Disorders). Basically any major negative shift in a child's behavior or attitude signals that something may be wrong or that something is bothering a child.

Look for extremes in a child's behaviors or swings from one way of being or relating to it's opposite.

B. PRINCIPALS OF WORKING WITH TRAMATIZED CHILDREN:

1). Do not be afraid to talk about, play out or target (when all other safety criteria and relationship needs are met) the traumatic event or events. Wait for the child to bring the event or events up in play. Formulate targets in "digestible steps or units," that lead up to the trauma that has brought the child into treatment when using EMDR. In other words, if the target is a person who has harmed the child, you may want to start with their clothing or their voice instead of their face, initially.

2). Provide safety, consistency, neutrality in your patterns of working with traumatized children. Toys in the playroom need to be consistently placed each time the child visits the room. Your voice, body-language and attitude toward the child should be the same, week to week or session to session. When using EMDR let the child have as much control and possible. Begin and end with installing "SAFE PLACE."

3). Be nurturing, comforting - be affectionate when you are sure the context is safe for the child - do not ever command a child to hug or kiss you. Ask before touching. Be careful to keep firm boundaries with traumatized children. Often, they have a poor understanding of personal boundaries because their boundaries have been violated.

During the play session, be who the child needs you to be; ask along the way for "role clarification" (during traumatic or intense re-enactment children generally direct the therapist to be in the perpetrator role - this type of play is difficult for some therapists please discussion to follow in the Working Stages of Play).

4). Set limits only when needed. Be clear and consistent. Respecting a limit is a child's choice, if the child chooses not to respect the limit, be clear about the consequence the child is choosing instead. For example, "If you choose to shoot that dart at me again, you choose to NOT play with that gun for today."

Children who are traumatized or have Reactive Attachment Disorder (RAD) need a lot more limits set for them during play because they need to learn two important lessons. The first lesson they need to learn is that you are emotionally stronger then they are (Safety and Trust) and the second lesson is self-control. (Self-esteem/lack of manipulation).

5). Go to the child's level when giving/receiving information - especially on a physical level. Greet the young child on your knees or while sitting or crouching down. Be honest - but keep it simple. It is a good idea to physically go to the child's level when talking/playing and try and maintain this non-verbal support. If the child wants you "bigger" they will let you know. Sometimes with RAD children, it is important to let them know you are "bigger" than they are because that will help them to feel safe.

6). Prepare (yourself) for re-enactment of trauma/abuse in play sessions and the re-experience during EMDR. Explicit acting out of sexual or other crimes perpetrated upon a child is upsetting. We are trained, as clinicians, to keep our feelings about that to ourselves. Often I tell the children I am very sorry they were hurt (or the baby doll was hurt)) - I always remind them that babies are never wrong and never cause the hurt to happen.

7). Protect the child: Teach the STOP commands before using EMDR. And STOP must always mean STOP. If the child refuses to continue EMDR at least get the child to go back to their safe place for a set of EM and then return to the play. Address the child's feelings of anger, fear (?) toward you or EMDR that may have arisen. If there is too much resistance, let the use of EMDR go until more information about the child can be obtained through parent interviews or through the play therapy sessions. Sometimes, given the freedom to choose, children will ask for the EMDR again.

In Play, let the child know that s/he is safe no matter what comes up in the play. Children need to know that you are able to and will, protect them from their emotions. They need to know you will still "like" them, no matter what they tell you either verbally or in the play. I always tell children this: "You know what? In here, you can never get into trouble, never."

8). In play sessions, the child is essentially in control of the play and leads the therapist. In EMDR the therapist leads more, but can give the child some control over the process. Empower the child to know that they can get stronger, make their power stronger and that these

11

"games" you play together help them do that. Children need more reassurance when using EMDR.

9). Traumatized children have been hurt. They have lost their dignity, their safety and their self-respect. Traumatized children are often, at baseline, in a state of low-level fear - a state of hyper-arousal - ready to move from calm (low-level fear) to alarm, often moving from fear to terror very quickly. Often the "triggers" are unknown to us initially. Be sensitive to these children's "always on alert system."

The brain chemistry of children with many early childhood stressors is being wired differently than the brain chemistry of a child who is in a nurturing environment - and not for the better. The tendency toward depression, learning disabilities and violent behavior in the future is laid down in the neuro-transmitters and synapses of the brain in the order and kind in which it is received. Indications and research indicate that between conception and the age of four and then five to ten years, before the onset of puberty, is the optimal window for learning. Learning in the sense of wiring the brain. And although we are always learning, the question is what are we learning? What has a child of trauma learned about herself and the world around her? How can experiential play therapy and EMDR help to create new, stronger and better wiring in the brain, mind and soul of children?

New neurological pathways can actually be created in the brain. "Foremost among the brain's operating rules, which have come to light only in the last five to ten years, is that it (the brain) constantly rewires itself, even in old age, changing physically and chemically in response to an individual's experience."

(Inside the Brain, etal., Ronald Kotulak, Andrews McMeel Pub. 1997 p. 131).

Further, neurobiologist Ronald Kalil of the University of Wisconsin determined that young animal brains are awash in chemicals called growth factors, while adult brains have far lower levels. He surmised that the abundance of growth factors helps the new brains organize themselves; when damage occurs, the growth factors simply start over and rebuild the damaged networks. (Ibid. p. 149).

"This organ that seemed so inaccessible, that seemed as if it couldn't be repaired just a few short years ago, now appears to be monumentally plastic, and we are beginning to take advantage of its healing powers," says Dr. Ira Black, chief of neuroscience and cell biology at the Robert Wood Medical School in Piscataway, New Jersey…. The key to the brain's plasticity is a newly discovered family of chemicals, including nerve growth factor, that keeps brain cells alive. They are called neurotrophic factors, from the Greek "neuro" for brain and "troph" for nourish…. The "super-nannies of the brain cells…." (Ibid, p. 151).

10). GO SLOW AND STEADY. Picture the child well and healthy when you think of them and encourage their parents to do the same. Focus on the child, not the problem.

The effects of violence and stress on kids' brains is considered a "new epidemic" that is ravaging our children. They are too often victims of bad experiences. These bad experiences causes brain damage. This damage can increase the risk of developing a wide variety of ills ranging from aggression, language failure, depression, immune-system dysfunction, and diabetes. Unfortunately, the problems that cause the development of diseased networks in the brain cells are on the rise.

"That puts a lot of importance on parenting because that has a big impact on the way the brain becomes wired," said Christopher Coe, a University of Wisconsin psychologist who has shown that infant monkeys deprived of parenting have deficiencies in key brain structures and suffer from numerous immunological disorders. "There is a social cost if you don't have good parenting. It may be that you stamp and individual for a lifetime, not only in terms of their behavior and emotions, but literally their predisposition for disease." (Ibid, p. 37).

THE PLAY OF THE CHILD WITH PTSD (Posttraumatic Stress Disorder):

Will range from inhibited to wild much like the play of the overly anxious child.

(See section on the anxious child). Their themes include: anger, helplessness, disempowerment, fear and they tend to re-enact the trauma over and over again in order to gain mastery over it once they feel strong enough to re-enact part or all of the actual traumatic event. Regressive behaviors usually emerge and these children *almost always* "get worse before they get better."

Children suffering from PTSD symptoms have a high need for control. Their play can become rigid, repetitive and the child may issue a stream of directives to the therapist asking to play a certain way. Often, a perpetrator role will emerge in the child's reenactment play.

During the intake process, I explain the Stages of Experiential Play based on Byron and Carol Norton's model, and "warn" parents of the commitment involved in bringing their child to therapy. I explain the strong possibility of regression and escalation of the very behaviors they are bringing their child to me to heal. I explain "nurturing discipline," and that it is better to work through the PTSD symptoms now and give the child relief.

SECTION 4: What needs to happen first?

After taking a through client history and the clinician has obtained the most comprehensive clinical picture of the child and the family, the pros and cons of using EMDR may be discussed. The family's stability is important to assess in terms of being able to support a child's likely emotional upheaval during the working stages of therapy. The working stages of therapy can be tough and exhausting; parents and children need a lot of support. Children need Nurturing Discipline during this time of extremes. (See Section on The Working Stages for explanation of Nurturing Discipline.

1). If at all possible, meet with the parent(s) alone. Obtain a thorough developmental history from the parents. It is advised to include a fairly comprehensive medical history. It is important to screen for medications, side effects of the medication(s), the child's feeling about taking medication as well as the parents' attitude about administering medications. It is important to screen for respiratory disorders such as asthma or seizures. Each history should include a detailed trauma history, behaviors that are concerning the parent and the context in which they occur. A child's fears, weaknesses, likes, dislikes, interests, strengths and abilities give the clinician a good base to work from.

Also assess the child's imaginative powers and understanding of fantasy and reality.

It is helpful to ask the parents how a child has mastered a developmental task and ask the child how it felt to learn/master a new task: (ie:) toilet training, learning to ride a bike, speech and/or sleep regulatory functions.

Assess the child's functional level prior to the traumatic event(s). Try and ascertain in what ways the child is still functioning well in the post-trauma period. (Can be accessed through parent stories).

More details on screening will be covered under "When NOT to use EMDR with children." (In Section 11).

2). Explain your training in working with children. Explain the basic stages of play therapy and the general course of treatment including what they may expect from the play therapy. Explain EMDR, your training in

EMDR, and the pros and cons of using EMDR along with the play. Explain why you may integrate the EMDR with the play for the child and give a brief description of how you might do that. Have them sign the consent form and make a brief documentation in your notes that this has taken place.

3). Ask the parents to bring the child in next time. They can tell the child that they are going somewhere "very special," to play with a (person) who likes to play with children. Often, older children have been in therapy before and do not want to come back. I usually ask that children come in to meet me before the sessions start when they are over the age of 9 years so they know right away that I respect their ability to choose and be part of the process. Sometimes it is better to leave the word "therapy" out especially with young children and children who do not want to re-enter therapy. "There is a (person) who just wants to play with you. You can see how you like it, ok?"

4). Older children/younger children: Generally, older children have a much better perspective on things and on the passing of time. They are generally more able to understand, accept and tolerate momentary discomfort and the reward that it will bring. Often, the adult protocol or a modified version of the adult protocol can be utilized with older children.

5). One way to introduce EMDR is by "parent demonstration," especially when the parent has been in therapy involving EMDR and have had a positive experience with it. Discuss the possibility with the parents before the child is present. Let the child watch the parent do EM.

6). Play is a wonderful form of therapy and playing before using EMDR facilitates using both play and EMDR simultaneously. As you discover the child's experience in the moment - in the present tense, for perhaps precious seconds of time..... you spontaneously apply bi-lateral brain stimulation with imaginative play, add your therapeutic, heartfelt responses and watch the child heal.... And watch your inner child heal also! (Discussed in Section 8).

SECTION 5: Informed Consent: It's part of the process:

On the following page is a sample form entitled: INFORMED CONSENT FOR EMDR. I use this form for both my child clients and adult clients. This form was developed after a period of trial and error. During that phase, I understood that only so much information pertaining to EMDR and children could be delivered to children and their parents initially. This form indicates two things: 1). *That EMDR will be explained before ever using it with any clients and* 2). *That EMDR 's explanation is an on-going process that may occur each week at the parent's request, child's request or therapist's discretion.* I have also written a two and a half page explanation about EMDR that I give to parent's to read along with an explanation of the play therapy process. (In back of book; available to copy.)

MELLENIUM NOTE: In 2001, a lot more of your clientele is aware of both play therapy and EMDR - but informed consent is not only constitutional, it's educational - and establishes nice, safe boundaries in an arena of respect.

If at all possible get BOTH legal guardians signatures. This is of particular importance when the parents are divorced or in disagreement as to the child receiving therapy. I make it a policy to contact the parent who does not bring their child to therapy to let them know that the other parent has brought their child to see me. It is vital to a court case that both parents have equal access to you as the therapist. If the custody is "joint" or termed instead " shared parenting responsibility," both parents MUST give their consent to treat the child at all and it is best if both parents are informed of your methods.

Even if the custody is "sole" or "sole parenting responsibility," it is a professional courtesy to inform the other parent of this event it the life of their child. This action also sets a precedence of the respect you will give to all of your clients and their parents. Unless a parent is abusive to their child or to you, they are to be included in the process. This action also communicates to the child and to the "system" that you are a neutral and unbiased therapist - particularly at the onset of treatment.

Take reports of maltreatment, etc. from divorcing parents with a grain of salt, initially. Divorcing parents, especially in a contested situation, will say

ANYTHING about the other parent. If you are working with children, consider seriously to educate yourself on the issues of parent alienation and parent alienation syndrome, (PAS).* Time may or may not reveal the truth regarding a conflicted situation. To best guard your relationship with the child, maintain that both parents are important to the child as far as you are concerned and treat them in a manner that communicates that you value then equally as the child does. Let a "Parenting Time/Parenting Responsibility" coordinator investigate the case.

Your job is to understand the situation from the child's point of view. It is rarely helpful to the child's emotional well-being for you to side with either parent. It is not helpful to the child for you to investigate allegations against the other parent.

It is not helpful for you to interrogate the child. BEING with the child is what is helpful.

* There is a difference between parent alienation and parent alienation syndrome, though the symptoms or what is observed in the children can be similar. The distinction between the two is that parental alienation focuses on how the alienating parent behaves toward the children and the targeted parent.

Parent alienation syndrome symptoms describe the child's behavior and attitudes toward the targeted parent *after* the child has been effectively programmed and severely alienated from the target parent.

- Parent alienation (PA) is "any constellation of behaviors, whether conscious or unconscious, that could evoke a disturbance in the relationship between a child and the other parent." This definition is different from parent alienation syndrome (PAS) originally coined by Dr. Richard Gardner in 1987: "A disturbance in which children are preoccupied with deprecation and criticism of a parent-denigration that is unjustified and/or exaggerated."

- (Douglas Darnall, Ph.D, <u>Divorce Casualties,</u> p. 3-4.)

SAMPLE FORM (on next page, please feel free to copy it).

INFORMED CONSENT FOR EMDR

Name of Organization_____

Therapists Name_____

Credentials_____

I, _____, have
discussed the use of EMDR, Eye-Movement Desensitization &
Reprocessing with, (Name of Clinician, Credentials). By signing this
release, I certify that I have been given a thorough explanation of EMDR
before my child or myself have received this potentially powerful method
of therapy and processing stressful events. I also understand that more
information may be given, if I need to ask, during the course of therapy.
My signature also confirms that I have the authority to permit the use of
EMDR with my child, _____.

I have been specifically advised of the following:

1). Distressing, unsolved memories may surface through the use of
EMDR.

2). Some clients may experience strong reactions during treatment
sessions, although children are more likely to "act out" in-between
sessions; these reactions may or may not have been anticipated - these
reactions may include emotional or physical sensations. Further, these
reactions tend to dissolve within a few days and more positive ways of
adapting can be installed in the next session.

3). This treatment approach has been widely validated by research
with civilian Post-Traumatic Stress Disorder (PTSD). Research on
other applications of EMDR remains continuous and current.

4). Integrating Play Therapy and EMDR with your child will ONLY
occur if your child is comfortable with this process.

_____
Signature of Parent/legal Guardian for minor Date

_____
Signature of Adult Client Date

SECTION 6: Integrating Stage One of Experiential Play Therapy and A Child's Safe Place in EMDR

First and foremost, the playroom is a safe place and the play therapist is to be a safe person. To ensure any kind of successful treatment with children, special attention is given at all times to creating a safe psychological/emotional environment.

EXPERIENTIAL PLAY THERAPY BASICS:

1). Kneel down when greeting a small child. Notice something special they are wearing (that they can see), and comment. Or just say, "Want to see the playroom?" or "Let's show Daddy the playroom together." (or) "I have a room full of special toys for you to play with, shall we show Mommy together?"

Most children will quickly drop their waiting room activities and accompany you with or without their parents to see a "room full of toys." It is not uncommon for children ages three years old and under to insist that a parent stays in the play room with them for one to four sessions. A child this young who goes willingly with you without a primary caretaker causes a "red flag" to spring up in my brain as a caution to watch for attachment problems.

When a child enters the playroom for the first time, often the parent is standing in the doorway. Note how the child approaches the room and the toys. If you think of the playroom as a metaphor for life, the way the child interacts with the playroom, toys, parent and therapist is a direct refection of how the child interacts in the world. It is helpful at this point for you to sit down in a small chair and talk to the child: "The toys are in here for you to play with. You can play with them almost anyway you want- as long as it's safe."

STAGE ONE OF PLAY: (Norton's Experiential Model) Exploratory Stage

Typically, the first stage of play therapy is the Exploration Stage. The child will check you and the toys out. The child will check you out to see if you are a safe person, if you mean what you said about playing and to see if you are emotionally stronger than they are. For example, "When she finds out I hit my sister a lot, will she still like/accept me?"

Levels of therapeutic responses from the clinician remain superficial observations that track the child in the present, wherever the child leads.

It is helpful during the initial intake to coach a parent on playroom behavior *prior* to having both parent and child in the playroom if they are there for therapy. If they are there for an assessment, I often let things unfold naturally to assess the parents usual interaction style with the child.

Coming into the playroom is a risk for the child. Often, a child's confidence is boosted after having taken this risk. Younger children may want the parent in playroom, older children, at this point, generally dismiss their parent and are ready to play alone with you.

The child is telling you a lot both verbally and/or non-verbally during the first session, but the therapist keeps comments on observations - but remember! - Make mental notes of what the child is telling you. You may "get" the metaphors or direct hits as to what is troubling the child but it is too soon for more than a superficial response. Keeping your responses on an observational level communicates to the child that you will keep the relationship safe.

Lately, I have seen more and more children enter the playroom and "go right into their play; - " my hypothesis being that as the world becomes more stressful and violent, the children see my playroom, sense where I am coming from and figure "ok, this will work out ok ...." And just start telling me what their lives are like. Frankly, most children living in 2001 and under a great deal of stress and pressure. Few have time to just play outside in an unstructured way that allows for exploration, growth and self-reliance. Adults seem to be "taking charge" or supervising their children's play more and more often.

I have learned from watching hundreds of children play that surprisingly, children are highly intelligent communicators, sharing many of the same concepts as adults do and "talk about these concepts in a comprehensive language." The difference is that children do not use too many words if they use any at all. The key to communicating with children lies in your non-verbal communication even to the most subtle flicker of the eyelashes. How you move your body and your facial expressions will communicate who you are to the child and how you perceive them much more loudly than what you say in words.

Reminder: Children and response latency: Children have a longer response time to events in their lives, particularly upsetting or traumatic events. It simply takes longer for them to process a situation; it can take up to 6-8 weeks for a reaction. Children often assume the opposite posture to how they are really feeling.

GOAL: Align with the child/let them know you are there, let them lead the way.

Begin to establish a safe, predictable environment for the child.

It is vital to introduce the child and the parent(s) to the possibility of utilizing EMDR during the course of therapy within the first three to four sessions. Again, flexibility in the intake process is called for. Most parents come in worried and upset about their children's behavior - too much information all at once can be overwhelming and therefore misunderstood or disregarded. I always mention the possibility of using EMDR and if the parent is not able to be receptive to this additional information during the initial intake then more information can be given during parent consultation time - concurrent with the beginning phases of treatment.

Only finding "safe place," and installing "safe place," occurs during the Exploratory Stage of Play which helps keep both the play therapy and the EMDR at a consistent interweave.

In her groundbreaking book on EMDR, the creator of this method addresses safe place with children: "Before attempting to target dysfunctional material, the clinician should make sure the child has a usable "safe place." A feeling of safety and assurance is induced in the child through the use of eye movement sets in the context of an actual positive experience. For example, the clinician might ask the child to remember a time when he was in control and felt good and might have the child imagine looking, feeling and acting in a positive way. As the child holds this scene in mind, the sets are repeated until the child feels happy or positive, as in the imagined scene...."). Eye Movement Desensitization and Reprocessing: Basic Principles, Protocols and Procedures, Francine Shapiro, The Guilford Press, 1995, p. 277.

I have also discovered that a child's safe place *can be real or imaginary or a combination of both and still be very effective.*

If the initial introduction/integration of EMDR is woven into the play session during the first or second session this is ideal as it becomes a normal and expected part of later sessions. The therapist uses ethical, clinical and "gut" considerations regarding the decision as to when to weave in the EMDR. It is better to weave in the EMDR early, no later than session three, whether it's ever used again or not. Children will not miss it and if they do, they will ask about it.

One day, a five-year-old girl who I had briefly introduced to EMDR in her second session entered the playroom and said: "I have a question. Remember you said you had a way of fixing bad dreams and making them better? I want to try that." This was her comment at the beginning of her eighth session and I only mentioned one other time briefly that this option was available to her. She kept that information quietly stored until she was ready to use it. We processed the fear related issues through her imagery of a re occurring nightmare about tornadoes. (This was a real fear. Her father was a tornado chaser). She endured a minute or two of intense fear and anxiety during the peak of the EMDR experience. When I checked in with her in the following weeks she reported that the fear (in her tummy and heart and head) had "gone." She no longer had the tornado nightmare in which she feared the loss of her father.

Sometimes EMDR is used only for the Safe Place or to install positive cognitions and beliefs about themselves. Blending these two therapies at the beginning of treatment is like an (inexpensive) insurance policy that provides a lot of protection for the child later. Introducing EMDR no later than the third session anchors the EMDR as a part of a safe playroom experience.

Never underestimate the wisdom and subtlety of children; the little girl with the "tornado nightmare," received the EMDR introduction and appeared disinterested during my explanation. But when she was ready to utilize the method, she let me know and processed her fears. Not only had she heard my explanation she understood it, thought about it and when she was ready, she requested my help using EMDR. Do not underestimate these children; they deserve our respect!

Giving the child a ten-minute warning that the session is ending, followed by a five-minute warning is typical in any play session. If a child is very young or very intensely involved in playing already, introduction of EMDR is postponed. They will be too busy to hear you and from their point of view, you are interrupting them.

If the child moves through the first stage of therapy very quickly or skips over it to perhaps, return later and moves right into their traumatic play, this indicates that their trauma or difficulties are very current, very present for them. In play therapy terms this is called "pressured play." Again, draw on all clinical inner resources before introducing something that is therapist directed. For a child who skips stage one, (sometimes they even skip stage two) it is wise to stop the play a few minutes sooner to get them grounded in reality before they leave that session.

EMDR's safe place can be used to cushion the emotional residue of the session and ground them in the present. Skipping the first two stages of play and entering the working stages immediately may be a signal to hold of on introducing EMDR. Often, once some of the emotional pressure is off of the child through the play experience, they will go back to Stage One and/or Stage Two. Be cautious and "dialed-in" to the child's needs when timing the introduction of EMDR.

For older, calmer children, or children who have a "break" in their play; it is a wonderful opportunity to introduce EMDR in a way that will enhance and compliment the play. Introducing the idea that for "a minute" or "for five minutes," we are going to do "something" a little different works well. Adding that - "this "something" will help you feel better and make your power stronger." Initially, this takes place about fifteen (15) minutes before the end of the session.

Generally, talking about a safe place - real or imagined or both - is a good way to start. Or talk about something positive about the child or the feeling of being in the playroom. Use any variety of toys, methods (see next section) to capture the child's attention for these few minutes. Introduce the eye movements, hand taps or clicks; some children prefer elliptical movements or the figure eight to the straight back and forth movement. Tell the child what a good job they did. Contrary to the neutral stance we often adopt in the play sessions, EMDR requires a lot of positive feedback from the therapist to the child about what a good job they are doing. Then give the ten-minute/five minute play warning. "Hey, great job! We have ten (10) more minutes left to play today."

Slowly building the use of EMDR into the play session as it occurs naturally in time, based on being sensitive to the child's needs and cues is the best way to maximize these two modalities simultaneously.

What children teach us in the first stage of experiential play is that most kids "walk their talk." Most children perceive language as a form of control. Even the brightest most articulate three-year old cannot compete linguistically with most adults. So many times I remind parents that after they ask their child a question to watch their non-verbal responses. It isn't that the child is ignoring your question, it is that they do not have the verbal language to answer you. They are answering you in the only language they have.

If a child has been diagnosed with Reactive Attachment Disorder (RAD) and is not older than 8 years old, experiential play therapy can be effective treatment.

I do not bring foster/adopt parents into the play room for attachment work unless the adoption is 99.9% secure or has already occurred. If the birth parent(s) have not terminated their parental rights, I feel it is a disservice to the child to foster a bond that may be broken. The only time I bring a foster parent or a foster/adopt parent into the playroom *before* adoption is final is to confront lying behaviors. (It is the only way to get to the truth).

When "playing" with RAD children, I have found that it is useful to set more limits. For example, because they need to learn self-control, I will say to them:

"The sand is for staying in the sandbox." This is a limit I would not set ordinarily. I generally will ask them to help clean up unless they are under three years old. Sometimes, I will say "no" to them in order to confront their need for control. Most of the aspects of experiential play therapy stay the same for RAD children but the balance between you being in control and them being in control needs to shift in order for them to learn what they need to learn. When a child is older than eight years old and has been diagnosed with RAD, play therapy can be a *supplemental* form of therapy to help them to become more organized and to help them improve their

Victoria McGuinness

self-esteem. However, for these children who are older, it is not recommended as a primary therapeutic intervention.

Section 7: STAGE TWO OF PLAY: (Norton's Experiential Model): Testing for Protection/Building EMDR into the Play Session: How to lower or erase a child's resistance to EMDR

"How will s/he act when s/he sees the "real me?" "Are you a safe person?" "Will you protect me from my feelings getting out of control?" (Are you stronger/wiser/braver than I am? (Right now?) These are the questions (formed or unformed) on the child's mind in the beginning of your new relationship.

As therapist, direct empathy to the child on a conscious level. All of your verbal and non-verbal behavior should communicate support and understanding. Testing for protection may involve aggressive behavior, irritating behavior or boundary pushing. For example, hurling the bop bag into toys and scattering toys all over the place, flinging sand all over the room, asking to take toys home.

These behaviors usually generate a really negative response from adults.

Set limits when needed. "The bop bag can be punched and kicked but not thrown." (My personal limit until I have a completely empty room!) This is an example of I-thou limit setting - this *is* a two-way relationship based on respect. It is *essential to recognize the motivation and feeling behind the child's behavior in order to set a limit that will make sense to the child.* Redirecting the action slightly usually helps things along. Testing for safety and boundaries may also involve asking to take toys home from the playroom - always affirm that that particular toy is important to the child but be firm in your stance that the "toys live here." It is the validation and consistency combined that let the child know you will keep them the child safe. "I can see that the toy is very important to you - you would like to take something from the playroom home. But the toys live here. You cannot take it home. It will be here for you when you come back."

During this stage therapeutic responses begin to move to reflect the projection of feelings and experiences onto the toys. In each stage, therapeutic responses can be verbal or non-verbal and kept in the metaphor style. In later stages, responses should deepen to reflect the relationships or events "played-out" by the child, the therapeutic

27

relationship itself and need to reflect the child's own feelings about these relationships or events.

Reminder: Respond to the *motivation* behind the behavior; validating the child's experience is the only way to change unwanted behaviors. For example, when hitting the bop bag the therapist does not want to reinforce aggression or violence and DOES NOT say "Yeah, kill 'em, kick 'em, etc." Studies on violence do not support evidence to show that "venting" over and over again changes the need for aggression. The therapist's goal is to break the connection between the negative feelings and the aggression. This is accomplished by responses such as:

"This one needs to know what it feels like to be hurt in the face." (Possible issues of identity) or "This one needs to know what it feels like to just have to take it."

(Issues of powerlessness). These therapeutic responses to the bop bag will be covered more completely in the "Working Stages."

Goal: Establishment of trust by demonstrating to the child that you are focused on them and not their unwanted behaviors. You demonstrate your total belief that the child has a good reason for their feelings and they only need to change their behaviors connected with those feelings.

Therapists do not always know when they are being tested for protection, but a good play therapist is always safe and always knows when the test has been passed because the relationship shifts and the child moves into the "working stages" of play therapy. It generally takes 3-4 sessions for the child to accept you as their therapist. But remember there are always exceptions to the general rule as mentioned in Section 6. Children with RAD will attempt to show you their best behavior... children with trust issues may take even longer to express their needs....

It is the therapist's duty to realize that children, in general, would rather play than "do EMDR." During the Second Stage of Play when the child is testing you to see if you are safe, in order to keep them safe, introducing EMDR calls for caution and creativity. In order to keep the option open of using EMDR at a later point in therapy, a light approach is best. If a child is clearly resistant to the idea, be content that you have mentioned it believing and knowing that if and when the child is interested, they will bring up the subject again.

The value of the trust and the quality of the relationship always supercedes "techniques." Letting go of finding a Safe Place may be of more value that trying to find it. It doesn't feel safe to be pressured into finding a safe place! Letting go of EMDR may be of more value than using it, especially for a very vulnerable child. Letting go of our hope to be able to utilize EMDR to help this child may be more valuable at this stage than using it. Establishing trust is the most important thing because nothing truly therapeutic will occur without trust. When the child sees that you are content to just introduce EMDR, that they at least know about it and are truly willing to just let them play - then you are building a trusting relationship. Nothing can have more importance than the establishment of trust.

Sometimes it is helpful to verbalize to the child: "Oh, you think this stuff is too weird and you just want to play. That is up to you. If you ever want to change your mind, that is ok too." Then LET GO!

If you sense ambivalence in the child regarding the use of EMDR - like they are intrigued - but not right now - right now they'd rather play - certain suggestions can be made over time. Noticing what toy or toys the child uses a lot can be a way to lower resistance to using EMDR, such as: "I notice you really care a lot about this baby (doll), maybe your baby would like to try something new sometime," or "This baby needs a lot of love because she is having bad dreams - maybe you can hold her on her lap while I play the drums for a minute and we can help the baby to feel safer." or (for older kids).... "I see you play with that frog a lot - if you ever change your mind about that weird stuff we talked about, you know that EMDR stuff, you can use that frog to make your power stronger."

I usually write the words EMDR out so the child can get the letters right.

SECTION 8: Techniques for Integrating Play Therapy & EMDR

Once you have established trust, more information about EMDR can be offered to the child. Sometimes I say in reference to the playroom: "Problems have a way of getting solved in this room/place." When we stop for our EMDR time (which becomes more flexible over time), after the establishment of trust, you can go a little deeper. "We have some time to go to your safe place; let's take a minute to go there." (Install safe place). "You were really mad at that guy today, (ie: pointing to the bop bag). Remember how you punched him right in the face? Remember how mad you felt? Where did you feel the maddest inside your body? Can you remember doing that, how it felt, what you were feeling/thinking and do some eye-movements? (Or whatever you're using). Good. Great. Use the bop bag to facilitate eye movements or have the child hit one side of the bop bag and the other (or offer to do this for them.) "You want this one to know how angry you are; and what it feels like to be hurt. " Then -"Blow up the picture of this one. " How does it feel now? (Install a new set of EM).

"That shark (abuser/perpetrator) really was scary today. It really scared the baby mouse! (victim /child). I wonder if you could help the mouse feel braver by holding it and letting mouse do some EM (or whatever) so s/he won't be so afraid of the shark?" Let's help the baby mouse."

A child's resistance to EMDR and need for control can be lowered by taking turns; taking turns with the mouse, for example, enhances the child's desire to engage in EM. The child's ability to take turns will also give you some idea of that child's level of impulse control. With RAD children, the child may just be keeping you at a distance. In other words, I will cooperate with you and "take turns," but I'm really just staying in control of the relationship. I'll never let you see my dark side. By cooperating on a superficial level, you will never get to the real me.

The child can choose a toy to stimulate EM (and this is often the preferred method by children) instead of using your fingers. Puppets work very well, and with younger children who have trouble crossing the mid-line, a puppet on each hand works better. I have found that some children like the sound of two drums, one on each side - I can drum the drum or they can. Older children love the thera-tapper (a helpful device that amounts to two "joy sticks" one held in each hand by a child to facilitate bi-lateral brain stimulation). I call it the "buzzy thing." Older children and adolescents like to lie down comfortably and hold the handles in each hand as opposed to using eye movements. This way, they can close their eyes and relax and for many children this seems to enhance their ability to visualize. The pillow, blanket &/or couch helps them to feel nurtured during the process.

If a child picks an animal or an important figure to them for processing, the toy can be used both as a facilitator for the EM and also as a projective device: "How fast does the frog want to go?" "Tell Mr. Frog when the feeling gets stronger." To overcome resistance say, "It's Mr. Frog's turn now." ("Using EMDR with Children," Ricky Greenwald, Psy.D.")

Practice using STOP: Children are always being told: "No!" "Don't" "Stop" in life by adults. It helps them to know that they are the ones who get to say "STOP" now. "Let's try it. You are the police/person, teacher, (it's the child's choice).... so when you (or Mr. Frog) want things to stop, say: "STOP." Hand gestures may be added. Often children will take the suggestion to wear a badge of authority, ie: a Sheriff's badge as a way of "proving" that they are in charge of the process. Instead of the child being able to use the stop control-command, you may find that they are back in their safe place instead. This is generally a signal that the material is too painful for the child to process or that they have dissociated. It is good to reinforce their control level by practicing the STOP signal whether they are able to utilize it or not. And may be wise at this point to re-enforce/re-install safe place and return to the play and leave the EMDR alone for a while.

A. Metaphors, Targets & Themes

REM sleep, VCR's and remote controls, lazer guns, swords, transformers, jumping toys, "picture game," STOP signs, roller coasters, movies, colored light, computer games, images of themselves in the future, bop bags, etc. are all examples of metaphors used by the child and the therapist to maintain the child's control over the EMDR process.

NOTE: Think about the use of the word "magic," when describing EMDR to children. Some parents have a dislike or suspicion of the use of this word. Also, we want the child to know that the healing power comes from inside of them and reinforce an internal locus of control. However, there are times that the use of the word magic is very effective with children under five. "We are going to do something that makes your magic/power stronger," is a great metaphor for children. Power may be a "safer" word for most children but some kids may not relate to the word "power," especially the 0-3 population. Lately, in 2001 I find that most little ones are well acquainted with the word "power."

1. TARGETS:

Pictures or images are the best medium for target selection. The child can recall, draw or paint the target, "picture." As the target is processed, the picture can change. When working with a 13 year-old with early childhood abuse issues that occurred before her adoption at age three, she drew her birth parents (target) on the black board. As the SUDS level lowered, she would erase and add to her target to reflect her level of processing.

As her therapist, I did not have to ask for numbers, her drawings told me her SUDS level. She also has been diagnosed with ADHD and has been on medication since she was a small child of 4 years of age. She calls the hyper feeling her "bugs." We mutually discovered that *all of her "bugs" were not due to ADHD* and that EMDR might help to calm her "bugs" down. Some of her "bugs" were caused by the unresolved early abuse she endured from her birth parents before her adoption at about 3 years of age.

She created "Bugsley" - a figure who represented her anxiety and some of her hyper-activity out of play-dough. She also created "Ooglie" - a creature who is smaller than "Bugsely," but able to take a stand against "Bugsley" and being a victim of anxiety. We used these client-created images to externalize and target her feelings to focus on during EM. This talented young client also used a figurine from my miniature collection to represent herself "in the future," to use in facilitating EM. This image of herself as an older teen in the future non-verbally reinforced the feeling of hope as well as creating a self-generated direction (goal) for herself and her desired identity.

Nightmares, bad dreams, night fears, memories - all can be used as focal points to "bring up the picture," or "imagine what happened," "see the bad guy," etc. Starting with the most recent or relevant image is a good idea because that is what the child will be thinking about.

I worked with a child who lost her dog after an extremely conflicted divorce after witnessing years of domestic violence. When her dog came up missing, the loss of her dog took precedence over her divorce/witness issues. Until she resolved some of her sadness and grieving over her lost pet, she could not directly address the loss of the rest of her family.

Paying attention to the messages delivered by the child in the first few minutes of play will provide themes for target selection. Children will often walk into the playroom, pick up a scary puppet, replace it and move into their play. They have told you, *fleetingly but importantly*, that they are going to tell you about something that frightens them. *Paying attention to children's non-verbal cues* is a key element in selecting targets and catching themes that will work for them.

The use of story narratives can provide triggers for targets and also help de-sensitize children to sensitive subjects. (See Section 15).

When specific or (discrete) targets are available, these are most effective with children.

2. SOME SPECIFIC TARGETS:

1 - Memories of traumatic events

2 - Images of the feared person

3 - Bad dreams

4 - Physical symptoms/sensations/reactions

5 - Symbolic toy or object

6 - Specific anxieties or fears

7 - Positive goals/ beliefs about self

8 - Best thing about self

9 - Best thing you learned today

10 - Positive installations only best for some children

11 - Part of story or character in story that "triggered" stress response

12 - Positive image of self in future

13 - Client generated figures/drawings/creations

14 - Sand tray image or story generated by client

15 - Image of actual lost pet or person

16 - Colors for feelings and rainbows to connect heart losses or separations

EM by self: Case Example

A 7 year-old-male used empty coke bottle, a purple squeeze ball stress reliever (which he called a "plum,") and other odd objects to control the pacing of his EM. He kept quite a bit of information to himself, although I usually knew what feeling he was working on. He benefited from EMDR as well as play and remained in control of the process. Staying in control was something he really needed to do because he was working through genuine feelings of powerless and lack of control in his life. He lost his father to cancer just as his little brother was being born. Then, his mother was diagnosed with cancer. A life situation like this would cause anyone to feel powerless and search for some way of exercising control wherever possible. This boy always referred to EMDR as "CPR" which was funny - but also lead to me thinking it was good to write the letters down for the kids. ("My therapist makes me do CPR when I go to see her?)

3. THEMES:

Theme development is an important part of target selection with children.

THEMES IN CHILDREN'S PLAY CAN INCLUDE:

Power/control, loss/isolation, boundaries/intrusion, empowerment/self-esteem, perpetration/victimization, nurturing/neglect, internal conflict, external conflict, construction-creation/destruction, painful relationships/ fear/ sadness/ anger/ humiliation/secrets/abandonment, trust/betrayal, confusion/rage, etc. Most themes for children (as well as adults) revolve around the number 2 - duality - which reflects our basic human condition including good vs. evil, strong vs. weak, and so on. I find that most children grapple with good vs. evil these days both "out there" and within. The child's unformed question being: "Am I good or bad?"

Always remember that during therapeutic growth (Stage Four of Norton's Model) and EMDR processing that a variety of positive themes also exist, including: empowerment, letting-go, new things, learning, positive self-attributes, new concepts, self-reliance, honesty, courage, being "seen," being recognized as an intelligent, evolved being. There *is* light at the end of the tunnel.

A good trauma history and relationship with the parents will help select specific traumas for target selection. The face of an abuser may make a good target selection for some children, or using the bop bag as a projective device to desensitize picturing the abuser's face may help. If the face of someone is too scary and frightening for the child, target the hair, clothes or shoes of the perpetrator.

Zeroing in on the representational memories and processing these memories may be sufficient. If there is a cluster of experiences attached to the target, asking questions such as: "What's another time you were hurt?" or "Can you think of something else that makes you mad/sad, etc?" or "Have you ever felt that way before?" after a processing set helps develop the theme and clear the channel. It is in this way that children sometimes need help to verbalize associated events and to "connect the dots."

Working backwards to develop a theme seems to work best with children. (Present to past; or Little "t" to Big "T"). Some children will want to jump right in and work on the Big T; this too, is up to the child. Conversely, in experiential play children often work from past to present after the immediately current issues are played out.

I have found that when helping a child to process "secondary trauma" such as being a witness to domestic violence, it is helpful to integrate any positive memories or experiences that child has about their parents or family as the SUDS level lowers. For example, I worked with the 9-year-old girl who lost her dog, she reduced her SAD SUDS from "way big" to "medium." She could not go back into the sadness the next time we were ready to process. So, instead, we focused on positive memories of when her parents were "cool."

We also installed her belief that she would be different than her parents when she becomes an adult. These positive cognitions included: "I am kind," and "I am happy," and "I am me!" Then she chose to play "Candy Land." Per parents report, they never played "Candy Land" with her as a young child although they had with her older brother. She repeatedly chose this game as one of the ways to re-work her developmental issues that occurred during the years of witnessing the violence in her family. During the following session, she was prepared to "go deeper" into the sadness and again and balanced it by playing (and winning) "Candy Land."

Sometimes during experiential play, as long as EMDR has been woven into the play effectively, the therapist can interrupt the play and creatively insert EMDR. This is one of those times when paying attention and being quick is essential.

The first time this occurred was with a young child of 4 years who was playing out family issues in the sand table. She had T-Rex coming to attack and eat up the mother pig and the baby pigs. I interrupted her play and said: "Think about that (T-Rex gobbling babies) and follow with your eyes. Very quickly, I moved T-Rex with a baby pig in its mouth back and forth. For a few seconds her SUDS level increased. I said, "Let the baby pig tell us when the scary feeling is stronger," as a way of processing her fear through the projective use of the toys. The baby pig became very frightened. This enabled me to know we had a very high SUDS level and needed to keep processing until the child (baby pig) was safe.

Spontaneous use of EMDR during play implies flexibility in getting a SUDS level, if one is obtained at all. (See Section "C"). Going back and forth from the play to the processing is powerfully dynamic and the relationship must be strong enough to sustain this kind of intense interplay.

After completing EMDR processing, expressive, therapeutic play is a good way to wind down. Conversely, after a very intense play session, re-installing the safe place with EMDR can be a good way to end the session. This helps to ground the child's emotions back into present time.

Some children do not want to disclose their target at all or fail/refuse to articulate it or draw it or represent it in any way. This does not mean that they can't focus on the target for processing or that EMDR cannot take place. It may be a silent request for privacy or an indication of shame. The therapist can say, "If you just want to think about the bad man, dream, event, that's ok, too. It's kind of like your diary, and you keep it locked - and hide the key in a safe place - so no one else can read it." Children of all ages appreciate your recognition for their silent request for privacy. Most children do not experience a lot of private moments in their life.

If things do not seem to be moving along, search for body sensations, associations or return temporarily to the play to generate new or better targets. This is where the use of sand, play-dough and other tactile mediums can concretize the feelings for the child. If the trauma occurred in a pre-verbal state, the child may only hold the memories in his or her body or be triggered by a sound or smell. Returning to the play often reveals the sensory aspects of a pre-verbal memory as well as the developmental stage in which it occurred.

Feelings and problems can be externalized and made concrete in the play process and with the help of the therapist, children can attach meanings to an object, picture texture sound or smell and process that. This method is discussed in using art and sand to create images for processing.

B. MEASURING SUDS & VoC'S WITH KIDS: IT'S DIFFERENT; IT'S SIMPLE

1. MEASURING SUDS

It's always a good idea to get some reading on a SUDS level after an EMDR/Play session or any other EMDR session. With children, this can be very simple and quick. Staying with this much of the adult protocol is useful just to become grounded in the progress of the processing that is generally intensified or completed in the play. This kind of feedback also teaches children self-awareness, a feeling of being in control and understanding what may be going on for them with all this!

Again, when working with children, flexibility and creativity are the keys to success. Sometimes, within the flow of play therapy, SUDS are not used at all, but SUDS can be measured while saying good-bye for the session, informally. For example, measuring SUDS can be as simple as asking, "How big was the feeling of (name feeling) when you came into the playroom today?" "How big is it now?" I have a "feelings chart" in the playroom, in the observation room and in my office. "Show me how you're feeling right now. Hum, I guess you feel a lot different now then you did before you got here today." Kids like to identify their feelings on the chart of faces. This brief exercise helps to link their therapeutic experience with *their* feelings and the transformation of their feelings. They learn that they *can change their thoughts and feelings!* This is a very valuable ability to learn and own in life.

A basic hand spread seems to be the most common SUDS measurement with young children. "Does it feel this scary (hands a few inches apart), or this scary (hands 12 or so inches apart) or really scary? (arms open wide). Older children may like to create their own way of measuring SUDS even using colors going from dark to light. "When I'm annoyed it's light red, when I'm very mad it's dark red." The themes a child develops after using EM will help to "measure" the SUDS level accurately for the child as will their affect and behavior and body language.

2. Measuirng VoC's

With children, particularly young children, this scale is rarely used in any way that resembles the adult protocol. Older children will verify that the SUDS are lower but will give you clues as to the accuracy of that when the positive statements are "measured." When successful, the child will be noticeably less anxious. They will laugh and smile, make positive statements about themselves or act in a way that exhibits more self-confidence. The easiest way to measure VoC with kids is to verbalize the positive cognition yourself to the child (with or without the parent present). The child's response will tell you how true s/he believes that statement to be. With young children I may say, "You are a lot braver now." Head nods in agreement, "I'm brave." The child's response will let me know how true this statement feels to them. With an older child I may say, "You really are feeling more attractive now." Again, they will let me know how true this statement feels to them. "Well, sometimes I do."

3. The PC's & NC'S

Whenever reprocessing is complete, the positive cognition is installed. Easy positive cognition can be offered to children, especially young children.

Positive cognition can be as simple as: "I am safe." "I am smart." "I am good," etc. Older children can come up with their own negative and positive cognition and it's always better to use child- constructed statements when available. The therapist can simply re-construct them into a workable unit.

Negative cognition also tend to be simple: "I'm stupid." "I'm bad." "It's my fault." "I'm scared." "I'm unlucky."

Often children will initially describe both NC's and PC's in terms of an external locus of control: "No one likes me." "My Dad hates me." "The teacher is mean to me."

Sometimes parents can provide their goal PC (positive belief) for their young child. "Remember you played with your sister all day and did not hit her one time. You are such a good sister and a good listener too." This can translate in to the positive belief for the child that: "I am a good listener. I am a good sister."

Using the child's cognition and picture will generally process best by turning the NC's and PC's from an external locus of control to an internal locus of control and thus creating more specific targets. Some children need a little more nudging to become aware of this than others. Letting go of the need to adhere to the adult protocol is essential in working with younger children. "No one likes me." will be changed to - "I am unlovable, or yukky" or something like that in order to balance with the positive cognition of "I am a lovey, or I'm cool."

SECTION: 9 - INTEGRATING STAGE THREE OF PLAY (Norton's Experiential Model): Working /Dependency Stage & EMDR's Processing Stage:

In play, after the therapist has "passed" the test for protection (which can re-occur at different stages of the therapy as more and more is played out or when secrets have been or are just about to be revealed,) the child moves into the dependency stage of therapy, where the work is. It is at this point that the therapist would move into targeting the trauma more directly or use targets that are directly related to the play for EMDR processing.

In the play sessions, the level of therapeutic responses from the therapist need to deepen in order to address affect and dramatic play events, "Yes, that's just the way it went," or "that's just how you remember it," generally leaving the feelings in the metaphor but commenting on the actual event, relationship or experience. "That must really hurt the baby!" or "that little truck is away from the other ones... all by itself.... it must be feeling very lonely." It is important to convey to the child that it is known that actual life events are being validated whenever possible without breaking the security of the play.

During any stage, but particularly this stage, developmental age may be indicated by the child's voice changes, choice of toys and bodily positions. As the child regresses back into the trauma, the play intensifies back to the level of pain/pressured play. It is easy to see the large amount of energy a child uses to express a certain traumatic event. It is easy to see how important expressing this event is.

As the child re-enacts her traumatic experiences she typically will put you in her position as victim...to get you to understand what she went through.... you take her role (as victim) and "be" with her in order to let her know that someone finally "gets it." Someone actually know what is was like to be her during that experience and does not judge her for it. Instead, the task is to validate the child's experience and communicate their innocence.

Do not use the child's real name during the working stages of play as the use of real names will break the security of the play. The goal is to protect the child's identity and the child's ego. If you call them by name when they are in the role of perpetrator and you are in *their role as victim* the whole point of the play experience will be lost – at least in that moment. A seemingly small mistake can harm the trust that has brought you to this point of exposure. Experiential play is used for rehearsal for life and re-working life's experiences. Stay with the therapeutic metaphor and the play will progress.

The primary goal of the working stages is to validate the child's feelings and "be" with the child emotionally in the experience. Experiential play allows the child to tell her story her way. The therapist expresses empathy for the child by reflecting their true position during an abusive event. This was usually experienced as an innocent victim. Our job is to let them know that we understand what they've been through without judging the resulting behaviors.

The working stages of therapy are very intense and like EMDR can and will make the child "get worse before they get better." At this point, much attention needs to be focused on the time in-between sessions and parental awareness of selected targets. Contact needs to be maintained not only with the parents but also with pre-schools, baby-sitters teachers, etc. so the child does not get punished for the negative behaviors that re-enactment can bring to the surface. I find it vitally important that children do not get punished for being brave enough to confront and work/play through their issues.

I use the initial intake session to explain that putting one's child in therapy is a commitment. I further explain that a strong commitment is necessary to live through the working stages of therapy. A parent needs to understand **ahead of time** that the behaviors they are bringing their child to you to change may very likely worsen during this stage of therapy. I explain that I may need releases of information to help the school stick with this child if and when the negative acting out increases at school temporarily. I also use this time to teach a bit about nurturing discipline that needs to happen at home and at school. I remind the parents that *they* will need extra support during this stage too.

Often, I find I am in a position of responsibility to direct parent, teachers or other caretakers to help discipline the child in a nurturing way during this intense stage of therapy. When the child misbehaves, acts-out, etc, I coach them to say something along the lines of the following: "I know you are playing some hard (scary, angry, etc) things in the playroom with (therapist's name), but it's still not ok to hurt your brother ... push Bobby off the swing .... (whatever negative behavior the child has engaged in.) The feelings are ALWAYS valid. The behaviors need sculpting and modifying by the adult. Sitting with a young child during a time-out to talk to him and explain to him why he is sitting there is advice I give day-care providers and teachers and parents all of the time. Really, what would that hurt? Especially during the working stages of experiential play therapy and EMDR. It is of vital importance that the child does not get *punished for working on his issues* or a lot of efforts will be lost.

Nurturing discipline involves the following steps:

1. Remove the child from other children, animals or toys that are upsetting him.

2. Get down to the child's eye level and validate the *feelings or motivation for the behavior.* "I know you are feeling very angry right now. It's ok to be angry, but it is NOT ok to hurt yourself or other people. Let's sit here for five minutes and calm down.

3. When the child is calm you can say: "It's hard to behave when you're feeling scared. What can you do next time to help you to remember that people aren't for hurting?"

4. It is also important that the child understands the consequences for their negative (and positive) behaviors *before* they engage in them. Otherwise it is "no fair," and it's not. "If you choose to keep bickering with your brother, you choose to loose TV privileges for tonight."

5. At home and at school, it is wise to clearly and plainly WRITE DOWN the rules of the home or the school. The "Rules" need to be read to the child(ren) and clearly displayed in a place where they can be seen. This eliminates any arguments about what the rules actually are so things stay fair for everyone. One of the first rules is to NOT deface the posted written rules!

6. It helps to write down consequences as well.

7. All "Rules" are based on mutual respect including respectful language *including body-language.*

Validating the intensity of the child's efforts in therapy eases the need to control the behavior. Again, "I know you are playing some really hard things with_____ in the playroom." The child's feelings are always acceptable; the behavior is not - that is the message to the child. Offering re-direction for anger is always advised. "It's ok to be mad, but it's not ok to hit so-and-so. When you feel angry, you can hit this." (pillow, bop bag, etc.)

After the child knows you have "heard" them, the play will produce a shift in roles, and you may be asked to play the part of the abuser, help "level" the perpetrator and be part of the actions needed to render the perpetrator ineffectual and re-empower the child. If the child felt ridiculed or humiliated by someone, the child will attempt to have that "person" feel the same way. When a child is hitting the bop bag for example or scribbling on it's face the correct therapeutic response is: "This one needs to know what it *feels like* to be hurt in the face." NOT "Punch him, hit him, kick him!"

Sometimes during the working stages a child will let all the air out of the bop bag. "This one needs to know what it *feels like* to be totally deflated... or to have no power at all. I wonder how this one likes it?" You can direct words to the bop bag/perpetrator such as: "Yeah, how do you like feeling stupid?" or "How do you like having your power taken away, huh? Like it? You really need to learn a lesson." Kids love these responses and these kinds of responses help to break the connection between the negative feelings and the aggressive behaviors. After a while, you will see the child loose interest in engaging in the bop bag this way.

Goal: To deflate the abuser's or event's power over the child and empower the child by validating the child's experience and allowing an environment in which the child can re-do his experience of a traumatic event.

Reminder: Children cannot lie in experiential play; clinician responses to aggression needs to be about what is motivating the aggression and not the behavior, a CALM voice is important to feedback aggression and traumatic memories. It is of great importance to realize that the therapists' main task when dealing with aggressive behaviors is to break the connection between the negative feelings that the child is experiencing and the brutal or aggressive behavior. When beating the bop bag for

43

example it's ok to say "that really hurts!" children like that.... but, to leave responses there will reinforce the aggression.

Although children cannot lie in experiential play, they CAN avoid issues especially when there are attachment problems. Children with certain levels of attachment problems will work hard to keep from truly connecting with you. They may avoid certain play themes partly because they are afraid of loosing control and partly because they may not know how to really connect with another person in a genuine way. Sometimes they simply have not developed the ability to use imaginative play because their brain chemistry and experiences have not allowed the creative process to take shape in their brains. In other words, the pathways for imagination have not been developed. For many reasons, experiential play therapy with or without EMDR is not always the primary choice for treating attachment disorders in children over seven years old. It can be a wonderful support to any other, more specific form of attachment work however. Experiential play therapy *is* an effective way for developing secure attachment with younger children when the parents are involved in each session.

During the working stages there will be grieving and loss. An accurate assumption made by experiential play therapists is that children know instinctively what good nurturing is. The feelings of anger and sadness that the child is experiencing are totally legitimate. They are also contagious. Parents will feel the same feelings when they realize what might have occurred, let's say, in a day care setting. It is important that parents are reminded that if perpetrators were easily recognizable, they WOULD NOT have placed their child in that day care. In other words, the goal is to support the parents humanness too.

Nevertheless, the child's feelings will still run something along the following lines; "You (the parent) didn't protect me or care for me the way I know it should be or should have been. I was being hurt in daycare and you didn't even know or believe me when I said I didn't want to go. You didn't care about me when you said bad things about my Dad."

Goal: "Be" with the child on every level.

It would NOT be wise to interrupt a child's intensive reenactment play to insert a set of EM. This is a time when the play just needs to continue. Installing the safe place at the end of the session may help mitigate the effects of re-enactment, calm the child down and reinforce the fact that they are safe now.

The child who lost her dog during the very conflicted divorce was able to break through her numbed-out feelings using EMDR. When asked what she wanted to "work on" that day with EMDR she said, "Shadow." (Not the dog's real name). Her father (the person who she witnessed beating both her mother and brother) had told her that Shadow had probably been eaten by a mountain lion. Obviously, this added to her distress and sky-rocketed her SUDS level regarding the loss of her dog. Conversely, her mother told her that Shadow was either in "doggie-heaven," or sitting by someone's fire, healing.

Neither of these adult explanations really comforted the child I'll call Kali. First she wanted to know if there really was a "doggie-heaven," or if after she died she would be in the same heaven as Shadow. I told her that I didn't know for sure, but I believed that wherever Shadow was - in heaven or in another home - that she could send her love from her heart to her dog's heart. We had used colored lights to soften the pain in her heart before this discussion emerged. She had described her heart as a big, black bowling ball earlier in the EMDR session and used first violet, then green then red light in and around her body to see how these color-feelings effected the big, black solid mass of bowling ball feeling. I asked her to tell me what happened when the light met the big, black bowling ball. Gradually, adding each additional color to surround her body and touch her sad heart (for which the big, black bowling ball was her metaphor) her "regular heart" was re-established.

Because I believe it to be true, I was able to convince Kali that no matter where Shadow was, she could connect with her. Kali could not imagine Shadow dead or in another person's home. She could only imagine Kali waiting eagerly at the front door for Kali to return home. So we "went with that." Notice how her solution differs dramatically from her parents' solutions. The typical adult response would be to NOT reinforce this "unreal" scenario. But it worked for Kali because it was Kali's solution.

Respecting *her process*, I suggested she first see Shadow waiting eagerly at the front door for her to return home. I reinforced how much she and her dog loved each other. She picked the color red to send love from her heart to Shadow's heart. After one set of EM she told me that the stream of light was "only up to the driveway." With another set of EM, her eyes welled up with tears and said that she had connected her heart with Shadow's. Her SUDS level measured at hands about one inch apart – medium stress. She felt happier and her numbness was gone. We agreed that her hands might never completely touch (totally neutral SUDS) because she would always be a little sad about the loss of Shadow.

After the eye-movements, she got up and found the strongest bat in which to beat up the bop bag for the remaining few minutes. I can only guess that this was her way of expressing her anger toward her father for telling her that Shadow had been eaten by a mountain lion or generalized anger at all the losses she had endured in her short life.

Children can use colors to describe feelings either alone or in connection to a specific feeling. I will ask for favorite colors and know these are good feelings. Using colors with children (and adults) really helps to process tough emotions. I'm beginning to believe that colors and feelings are naturally intertwined in children's processing. It is easy for children to identify a feeling with a color and if they don't know the feeling they can almost always choose a color and tell you if they like that color or not.

A. USING ART & SAND TO CREATE IMAGES FOR PROCESSING:

The use of drawing images for processing has been discussed so much that this section will focus on the tactile experiences of sand, play dough and water. These mediums are always available to the child in the playroom where most of the processing takes place, be it through play or using EMDR. Children are tactile learners and much is learned and integrated into their belief systems using hands-on methods.

Children naturally gravitate toward sand and water during play sessions. Sand and water are elements that express the unconscious and unformed contents of the mind as perfectly as any medium in nature. The use of sand almost always conveys the feeling content of a child's psyche.

One of the best experiences of using a tactile medium to concretize feelings occurred with four year old Zack, (fictitious name) water and play-dough. He had been brought into treatment because of the difficulty he was experiencing trying to adjust to his parent's divorce and the relationships that developed as an outcome of the divorce.

Zack used a lot of sand in his play with and without water. He also used a lot of water, with and without sand.

Zack had made considerable progress in therapy and most of his symptoms had disappeared. But one day as we were moving toward the termination stage of therapy, Zack was a little down in the dumps. He got out the play-dough and dumped several colors onto the table. Little by little he added water to the play-dough as I watched. The water transformed the consistency of the play-dough into "slimey, yukky, icky," stuff. Together, our hands mucked around in these "slimey, gooey, sticky," feelings.... which Zack laid out on the table, so to speak.... This play enabled us to clearly identify some of his most negative emotions concerning recent divorcing family events which *were: "slimey, gooey, icky, sticky, and yukky."* Ok. Zack, now follow my (sticky) fingers and tell me what you feel now? "Good, glopey good!"

His negative feelings quickly yielded to laughter. We shared a "joke," at a time when therapeutic themes could have been very gloomy indeed. Not only did Zack understand the alchemical nature of water instinctively, he was able to process troubling feelings in a fun and very precise way. This experience was one of my first spontaneous instances of integrating play and EM. The EM in this case helped to validate not only his feelings but his ability to express and change his own feelings, his own way.

Children create sand tray pictures - which are really more like the "movies," or motion pictures - because most of the time children's sand play is in motion, processing. Dinosaurs fight viciously, threatening to take over the "water hole" of the lions, (survival themes) who try and defend and protect their babies from a large T-Rex who reaches down and grabs a baby cub between its sharp teeth and starts chomping. The big lion growls and bites T-Rex's tail, but the baby cub is hurt - no matter how, the metaphor will evolve.

Staying physically close to the sand table allows not only a close viewing of the dramatic action but also the child's expressions. I am almost always on my knees or sitting on a child-size chair. This is not a good time to be towering above the sand table looking down at a child's play.

I observe the play aloud saying: "The mom can't find her baby. Sharp-tooth is eating her baby...." I grab a "friend" dinosaur in my hand. "Quick! Watch this one; he wants to help the baby! Make the baby cry when the teeth sink in!" With luck, timing and practice... a short set of Em can be integrated into the sand play drama. "Mom is getting stronger - she's winning over Sharp-tooth!" (EM to reinforce safety.) When the big tiger attacks T-Rex with renewed strength and determination the dinosaur friend helps. T-Rex drops the baby cub. "Now, the baby is free and safe. " (EM). (It is important to use the word "safe" a lot in both EMDR and Play.) The big tiger picks up the cub and retreats to the corner of the sand tray. They -- safe right now. Then T-Rex falls on his back and is dead.

"The tiger mom and the baby cub are safe for now. They have a safe place too." Use EM with mom tiger and baby to reinforce safety and lower SUDS. "This guy wants to go too, watch him now so he can be safe to." Quick set using the same "friend" dinosaur or the baby and mom.

Here is where the real flexibility and creativity enter the processing. NC's are symbolically interpreted through the metaphor of the play. When T-Rex grips the baby cub between its sharp teeth it is easy to see the negative beliefs: "I am not safe," "I am in danger," "I am scared." As the conflict and fear are played out: The PC - "I am safe," is installed spontaneously during the play using the toys to carry the feeling. Later, the PC of "I am safe," can be re-enforced in whatever way seems most natural.

Usually, this type of play continues and the repetition of the theme will ensue. Just when we think everything is okay, T-Rex gets up again.... Roaring! This is the child's way of showing you the repeated nature of the abuse or fear. It appears that the integration of EMDR at these crucial moments may lessen the need for repetitive play in some children. In other words, the use of EMDR can help the child to feel resolution more quickly over repeated, traumatic events.

Art, sand and water modalities are applicable to children of all ages (including adults). This form of play therapy is particularly useful for children whose language development or skills cannot pinpoint the subtleties or intensities of their emotions and feelings. Tremendous relief is achieved by the externalization of strong feelings.

Play-dough or clay enhances the play by providing a clear expression for creation/destruction themes that are safe and within the limits of the playroom and toleration for destruction. Fantasy bombs, fantasy food or people or whatever is molded by the child provide an element of realism, being grounded and creative in a three-dimensional world small enough for the child to keep, kill, smash, obliterate or pull apart piece by piece. Play-dough or clay are often representative of a child's perception of their environment on a symbolic level. It is helpful to consider this symbolic meaning when a child picks up play-dough or clay in a session to see if it fits.

Any and all play therapy methods help convert the child's speech into the "language of play" and the integration of EMDR helps to take the processing further and deeper into the being of the child. One astonishing fact that I have discovered after years of being with children is this: Most children are *just as good at communicating as adults are, they simply lack the verbal vocabulary. It is the <u>adults</u> <u>who</u> <u>cannot</u> <u>effectively</u> <u>communicate</u> <u>with</u> <u>the</u> <u>child.</u>* Obviously, a young child who has a genius I.Q. does not command the verbal language of an even average adult. So, it is upon the adult to learn to communicate effectively with the child.

I am astonished at the young child's ability to form concepts and communicate them accurately as so are the adults who tune in and see it for themselves.

On little boy who just turned three and who had lived in a car with his mother who was a prostitute used this simple metaphor to show how the men in his mother's life took his place. He laid the male figures on a changing table for babies – he was literally explaining without words, "This man is where I'm supposed to be." It may be difficult to believe but it's true. It's also very important that adults begin to believe and know this about the children they spend time with.

SECTION 10: Where do siblings and parents fit in?

A. SIBLINGS:

Parents typically bring one child into treatment and that child's behavior is the focus of concern. As therapy continues, another child in the family may indicate the need for therapy. Sometimes the parents are so thrilled with the results ov therapy, they decide to "fix all of them." The child in therapy will occasionally request that a sibling be present in their session. I do not encourage this very often.

Even less often, simultaneous treatment of siblings will occur - weaving in alternating "alone," sessions and "together sessions." Most often, I will see siblings back-to-back for sessions. Personally, I have not experienced a problem with jealousy or rivalry between siblings with back-to-back sessions. The main reason for this structure is practical. If a family has two or three children in family most will choose to come to the office one time a week instead of two or three in the interest of time. I leave the deciding of who goes first, etc. up to the family.

Several considerations for choosing the appropriate treatment of siblings could be considered:

1). Age differences and role or position in the family structure.

2). Individual effects of (shared trauma) on each child.

3). Relationship with each other: competitive, protective, parentified, dependent.

4). Does the sibling enhance or detract from:

a). Child-client #1's ability to play out experiences?

b). Is child-client #2 so different from child-client #1 that the play is too chaotic or becomes less productive?

c). Does child-client #1 need the sibling to feel safe to process or to avoid the process altogether?

d). Will child-client #2 be traumatized by witnessing the traumatic play of the sibling or child-client #1 or vise versa?

e). Will child-clients loose or gain something valuable to the experience by the other's presence?

f). If child-client #1 was "first," will s/he feel like s/he has to "share even this?" Or loose the sense of being special in the relationship?

Whether or not to include siblings together in the playroom calls for clinical discernment and thoughtful judgment. I have not "experimented" with EMDR being used in the presence of siblings and have not seen any research to support the benefits of using EMDR in the presence of a sibling.

When integrating Play and EMDR, the decision of sibling inclusion is part of the overall treatment plan. Bear in mind that inclusion of a sibling may limit the use of spontaneous EMDR sets, which as discussed, can be very effective. In general, experience has shown me that in most cases sibling sessions are NOT productive unless the issues they are being brought in for require some relationship resolution between them. Even then, I will work with each child individually in order to understand their unique perceptions and to see how the session themes and activities change in the other's presence.

Older siblings can sometimes be encouraged to act as an EMDR "demonstration model" if the parents are unavailable or if the older child has been treated with EMDR and has had a positive experience.

A loved and respected sibling can provide material for cognitive interweaves as can best friends. But they do not need to be physically present in order to provide this material. "You think it's your fault that your parents are getting divorced. Is it Bobby's (sibling or friend) fault that his parent's are getting divorced too?" "No, you're pretty sure it's not. Well, just think about that..." Perform the EM to reinforce that knowledge.

Or: "Even after you really tried to (accomplish a goal) it didn't work. You're being kind of mean to yourself about that. If (beloved sibling or friend's name) tried that hard to do something and it didn't work, would you be that mean to them?" "No? Just you? No fair to you. I want you to think about that....." EM.

B. PARENTS:

The need for parental support has already been emphasized. Hopefully, it is clear that the more a child has her parent's support for therapy and feelings the better the child will do. Therapy will also go a whole lot faster and be more meaningful for everyone with parental involvement.

When using experiential play and/or EMDR with kids, most children are allowed access to their parent at all times. For very young children, parent access is always allowed when needed. Frequently, the parent who brings the child to therapy will be invited in the playroom by the child, at least for the first few sessions.

It is generally a goal of therapy to have the child be in the playroom independently, unless there are primary attachment issues that need to be addressed. It is not unusual to begin EMDR or Play for young children with the parent present. Often, little ones who are only two and three years old will only try the "game," of EMDR when securely placed on a parent's lap. And they usually need to make sure you are ok before dismissing their parent to play. Usually, after the trusting relationship has been established with the therapist, even the younger children will be fine interacting with you alone. It is important for the parents of young children to wait somewhere so that the child can locate them if they need to, reinforcing the safety needs of the child.

NOTE:The exception to this is when there is some attachment work that needs to be done. In that case, the parent is included in the play sessions until secure attachment is achieved and then the process of healthy individuation can begin. Attachment work in the playroom is best supported when paralleled by specific parenting and discipline systems at home. Attachment therapy may not be truly effective or successful without this combination.

Older children with severe attachment issues should not be in charge of whether their parent(s) come into the playroom with them until and unless that primary issues is healed. This is quite contrary to basic play therapy philosophy where the child chooses many of these dynamics. However, in order to **really help** a child with RAD, regular rules cannot apply until the most secure attachment is achieved. Even then, regular play philosophy needs to unfold slowly, one step at a time, with safety checks along the way. When true attachment is secure, then the play sessions can be engaged in with more alignment to the basic philosophy of experiential play therapy.

Older children generally do not wish to have their parents in the playroom at all, or will sometimes invite them in at the end to see something that they made, dressed up as, re-enactment of a fearful memory emerging etc. It can be a clear signal of social/emotional developmental delays when a child over four years old refuses to play alone. Although, sometimes the child just wants to "tell" their parent something in the playroom and is counting on you to "translate." In these cases, the insistence to have the parent present feels less pressured and once the child has "told" the parent what she wants them to know, they are generally dismissed by the child.

For example, 7 year old Anna (not her real name) wanted her mother to see her in a hooded black gown, face invisible, holding a knife tightly between her chest and arm. Anna sat calmly on the couch in the office and waited for her mother to come in. Needless to say, her mother was shocked and frightened at the image her daughter created for her mother to see. But Anna felt it was important that her mother be made aware of her emerging fears. Anna lacked the words but not the ability to communicate. I doubt that words could have conveyed the full frightening nature of the child's experience as well as the child's created metaphor did. Her action also communicated the importance of her mother knowing her emotional experience.

In a very real sense, she shocked her mother into facing her darkest fears by graphically demonstrating them. Anna needed her mother to be aware of her inner world of terror. Her mother was jolted into making some positive changes in her handling of a very conflicted divorce for the benefit of her child.

With children over seven years old, integrating a longer session of EMDR into the play sessions seems to evolve naturally over time. A good way to break down the session is to include 20 minutes of EMDR and 30 minutes of play. The child chooses which will happen first, EMDR or Play because they may have limited control over how long each section will last. Older children enjoy fair negotiations in which they can decide time-slots for dividing EMDR and Play or the use of alternating sessions. "This week I'll do EMDR, next week I'll play." Not only is this empowering and helps the child to take control of his or her own healing process, it reinforces the therapist's faith in the child's innate ability to move toward wholeness.

Negotiating, reward-setting and other motivators for EMDR evolve over time with the strengthening of the therapeutic relationship. Some older children prefer EMDR rather than play and are fascinated by the process and will request EMDR sessions primarily, especially when given the choice. The truth is though, if you have a wonderful playroom with toys, the majority of children will vote to play rather than engage in EMDR. Even a few minutes of a play session enhanced by EMDR is very worthwhile.

Obviously, in most cases and with most parents the stronger the alliance with the parents, the better. When parents are distant and/or uninvolved in their child's therapy it is an issue that needs to be addressed in some way based on the best interest of the child. Parents tend to be: involved, over-involved, under-involved, neutral.

However parents present initially, it is important to remember that the parental issues are often what brought the child to therapy in the first place and that the interplay between parental disturbance and the child's issues is generally a positive correlation.

If one of the parents is opposed to their child being in therapy, this can create a conflict for the child. Depending on the parental level of resistance, if this resistance cannot be overcome, use clinical discernment to decide if you are still the best therapist for this child. In cases of divorce where there is shared parenting responsibility (joint custody) you must have BOTH parents agree to you as their child's therapist and you need to have BOTH parents complete your paperwork, sign your mandatory disclosure statement and so on.

If one parent has sole parenting responsibility and the other parent has only been awarded visitation, it is helpful to the child to let the other parent know that their child is in therapy with you. If a case goes to court and one of the parents has not been informed of their child's therapy, you will appear biased.

In the case of proven perpetrators or abusers who generally, hopefully do not have unsupervised access to the child I will then choose to

54

communicate to the person providing the supervision. The motivation for this communication is to facilitate any healing that may be possible.

SECTION 11: When Not to Use EMDR

When there is no agreement on a specific target; it is not time for EMDR.

Most children are quick to agree upon a target that makes sense to them. Sometimes, only positive installations are selected, agreed upon and installed.

Sometimes, only the safe place is installed. When there is no safe place, it is not time to use EMDR unless it is deemed therapeutically important to "find" a safe place for the child once the trusting relationship has been fully established.

I tell children this: "We are going to start with your Safe Place. This place can be real or imaginary or a combination of both. This safe place needs to be a place where you are *totally safe and totally comfortable where* **nothing bad** can happen to you." Most children, unless they are so traumatized that they cannot even imagine being safe, can create a safe place. If they can't, use the play to build trust. Do not use EMDR if the resistance is too high or there is no safe place to install using EM.

"Anna Freud refers to children's inability or unwillingness to embark on free association, their unreliable treatment alliance, their diminished sincerity and frustration tolerance, and their preponderance of action as opposed to verbal expression. All these characteristics of children can contribute to resistance in child therapy..... Anna Freud compares and contrasts the adult and child patient, noting that while the resistances of the adult are lodged in the id, the ego, or the transference, the bulk of children's resistances "stems from their ego's age adequate preference for clinging to its own methods for safeguarding or reinstating well-being and for their inclination to reject all others." (Clinical Work with Children, Judith Mishne, 1983 p.298).

1. RESISTANT CHILDREN:

Resistance is not merely a basic unwillingness to participate in treatment - it is generally defined as the opposition that develops in the course of the treatment as a consequence of the treatment process.... and the content of internal conflict to be defended against. In the course of play, children dramatize their defenses quite literally with toy armor covering the chest or heart, helmets to protect their heads, swords and guns used to ward off or indicate pain.... because the theory behind play therapy involves a built-in mechanism for protecting the child's ego through the use of symbolic toys on which to project their defenses and feelings, resistance to play therapy for more than three or four sessions is rare unless the therapist themselves damages the safety of the relationship.

Most children who are resistant to EMDR are so because they are either not ready to tolerate strong, painful emotions, have trouble with trust, are too young, have had negative therapy experiences before, are rebelling against parental wishes or just don't like/trust the therapist or are suspicious of the "weird" stuff called EMDR.

I have not met a child yet, even as old as 13 years who has been resistant to the playroom. Even older kids, say 11 or 12, may be shy, fearful or "cool," they tend to pick games that don't seem babyish and ignore the other toys in the playroom (initially). They may sense or be afraid that someone (the adults) is trying to make them into the child that the parent desires. Latency-age children generally share a reluctance to share private thoughts and personal feelings.

Confidentiality concerning the child's self expression and what is shared with the parent's is an issue that needs to be openly discussed with the child and the parents. Often, older children are caught between telling the therapist something negative about the parental relationship and remaining loyal to the parent.

Children and their parents need to understand the limits and boundaries of confidentiality from the beginning. The fact that therapists are bound by certain legal obligations that supersede the obligations of confidentiality needs to be shared from the beginning. Parents are informed of this when they sign the mandatory disclosure statement you provide for them. I will not even take a child into the playroom without having this form signed by at least one legal guardian.

Confidentiality can be explained to children in language that the child can understand. "Just about everything we play or we talk about in here is between you and me, it's private. I won't tell anyone anything unless I get worried. I will get worried if I think someone might be hurting you, or that you might be hurting yourself or someone else. My job is to help you feel safe and be protected from scary or hurtful things or people. So, I'll tell you if I feel worried that something bad is happening to you and who I will need to talk to about it."

Since traumatized children have been betrayed it is important, actually crucial that they do not feel betrayed by you. Do not reassure that child that "everything will be ok," if and when abuse is reported. Never promise that a certain desired outcome will be obtained. Focus on your role as healer and offer the child a vehicle to digest what you have just told them. The playroom and sand trays are wonderful options for processing these kinds of communications.

Offering the sand tray and the miniatures within or outside of the playroom often helps the latency aged and pre-adolescent child find a happy medium with self-expression because they do not have to verbalize at all if they don't want to. Yet, a plethora of information is being offered through the creation of a sand tray right before the therapist's eyes.

When resistance diminishes, these sand pictures can be used for identifying targets for EMDR processing. Resistance is a defense and defenses that have been constructed by traumatized children are always to be respected. When the child senses that they no longer need that defense with you, they will drop it, at least while they are with you.

When a child is resistant to any aspect of therapy, my belief is that it is past experiences, parent presentation of what will be happening and expected of the child during therapy, the stigma of therapy and the therapist's approach are the main causes of resistance in younger people. More importantly, a child's resistance may be a signal that they have been threatened to "not tell anyone," about something that has happened to them.

I believe that resistance needs to be respected by the therapist. Basically, it is up to the clinician to soften the barriers to treatment by relating to the young person in the way they need to be related to. The first rule of thumb being to accept the child *exactly as they are with no need to change them, "fix them," etc.* Sometimes, this is easier said than done. Engaging the parents as co-therapists and educating them about their child's resistance, will, in most cases, take care of it with a young population of clients.

Until a therapeutic bond is formed and trust is established, don't push. It is not likely that any form of therapy will help until the initial barriers are dissolved. There may be parental pressure for "something to happen or unwanted behaviors to change." Economics and the inefficiency of the managed care system can be pressuring the parents leading to a vicious cycle of frustration.

The fact that you, the therapist, are paid to "care for the child," is not lost on young children and is certainly not lost on older children. "I'm sure you wouldn't care about me if my parents didn't pay you to," can be an underlying factor of resistance in older children. Accurate self-assessment and honest soul searching as to whether you are the best therapist for the child is essential. Just taking your time - or letting the child take his or her time, is therapeutic and gainful. It's worth the time and effort to explain this to parents.

There always seems to be a way to reach a young person when the goal is to do just that unless there is a more severe diagnosis that should be treated in a different treatment setting altogether. Playing games or offering the opportunity to "make pictures in the sand" will often soften the resistance. In short, moving the intense focus off the resistant child will tend to break down the barriers to treatment.

Sometimes EMDR can be used to measure and lessen resistance in older children: Using the resistance to therapy, even to EMDR as a target. For example, "How much or (how big) do you hate therapy/EMDR?" Slowly, in bits and pieces EMDR can be integrated to measure the older child's resistance and little by little curiosity and trust will override the child's fears.

EMDR and PLAY can be used with resistant clients - and can be used effectively to reduce resistance. Reminder: "It takes a lot of slow to grow." (Landreth, Garry)

In my experience most children are *not* resistant to therapy unless they have had a very negative experience with the system, a therapist or if one parent criticizes the need for therapy. Play therapy rooms should be very inviting to the child and will communicate almost immediately to the child that this room was created for them. It is important to be able to perceive when you are being tested after therapy has started. For example, I see a five year old child who has been in multiple placements. The last placement removed her from her three year old sister and she lives with an 11 year old foster brother who resents living with her because he was removed from his sibling.

Shortly after enough trust was established for her to be in the working stages, two social workers who manage her case came to the home to visit. This little girl perceives them as the people who keep her from her sister. So, during her next visit with me she disagreed with all of my observations and comments. If I had misunderstood her motivation, which was to test me to see if I was still a safe person, I would have created resistance. What I said was: "Gee, I just can't say anything right today," and "You just want to say no to me a lot today, that's ok." After about a half-hour, she was back in the safe groove again.

A mistake therapists make when working with traumatized children is to expect them to verbalize about what has happened to them. A trained play therapist will know that the child *is "talking" to them about the abuse through their reenactment play* and will not be frustrated by this. Needing the child to verbalize about their abuse will create resistance.

The less intrusive you are as the child's therapist, the less resistance you will encounter. When you treat a child with genuine regard and respect you will receive the same treatment in return unless the child is so disturbed that they should not be your client for these forms of treatment at all.

2. DISSOCIATIVE DISORDERS IN CHILDREN

Dissociative Identity Disorder (formerly Multiple Personality Disorder in DSM III-Revised) is generally assumed to begin in childhood. Dissociation may be manifested by the child who is in a trance-like state, who may experience amnestic periods or fluctuations in behavior that cause marked disruption to the child's ability to function.

Dissociation is a "split" from the reality of the present, and is often developed as a way of coping and surviving the trauma or effects from the trauma. Dissociative states can become "parts" of a trauma victim's personality. Personalities, sub-personalities, alternate personalities are created or developed to cope with trauma, as a result of trauma and to carry the worst of the memories and usually begin in childhood. (Putnum 1991).

There is still no concrete agreement as to what "personality" actually is. Are we the sum of our parts or greater than the sum of our parts? Are we the sum total of our experiences and memories? Or are we more than that? There is agreement that "personality" is the stable core of who the person is, the summary of <u>consistent</u> <u>ways</u> a person thinks, feels and behaves. Since the primary personality structure is formed during childhood, dissociative disorders are almost always reported as beginning in childhood by adults with this disorder. Dissociation is a natural state of mind defined on a continuum of intensity, frequency and duration. When dissociation moves from, "I completely forgot to take the chicken out of the freezer," to "I can't remember my teacher's name or what I did this morning," – red flags begin to fly.

Dissociation is a common feature of trauma survivors. Braun (1988), describes his BASK model, explaining that the main steam of consciousness is made up of four processes – Behavior, Affect, Sensation and Knowledge-functioning along a time continuum. When the integral BASK components are consistently congruent over time, consciousness is stable and the mental processes is healthy. Braun asserts that "the goal of psychotherapy is to obtain congruence across the BASK dimensions in space/time, thus yielding a decrease of dissociated thought processes, a decreased need for the defense of dissociation, and more control over interactions with the environment." (p.23).

EMDR can be used with children who suffer from this disorder when properly prepared to re-experience the trauma. Children can identify uncomfortable body sensations fairly easily and give them colors... black, gray, brown, etc. and focus on them for even brief periods of processing. Negative cognitions such as "I am scared." "I am alone..., mad, etc." can be targeted. Using EMDR to teach children over seven years old to step back and see that the negative beliefs and feelings are associated with a disturbing event or person helps them to separate the negativity from themselves. They learn that perceptions can change.

The alignment of target selection appears to be consistent with the BASK model of dissociation posited by Braum (1988).

Interpretation of child's behavior in the playroom:

The disordered or abused child may ignore you, their therapist. Often their body language will exclude you – they may play with their backs facing you. There will be little direct eye contact with you, especially on your terms.

The behavior of the disordered child tends to polarize from ignoring you or being uncomfortable with you to instant over involvement with you. They may indicate dependency by asking questions they already know the answers to and insist that you decide what will be played. You will feel the tension that is created by the inner conflicted needs of the child: I want to control you; I want to be close to you. Their play is pressured, often disorganized, their movements intense or choppy. Their play is often repetitive, using the same toys in the same way over and over again. Themes other than chaos are difficult to determine because the child's play will lack a consistent pattern.

In the playroom you will see frequent and abrupt shifts in their play with a string of uncompleted themes or scenarios scattered unfinished around the room. Often they are careless, discarding toys the way they feel they have been discarded. Sometimes, they just "zone-out" or appear to be in a "trance" as they re-enact a trauma.

There are similarities in the play of children with Dissociative Identity Disorder and Reactive Attachment Disorder. The most common similarity is the polarized way you are treated and the way these children "talk" verbally or non-verbally about their caretakers, past, present and future.

The behavior of these children often include a lot of limit setting and constant reminders of "We don't hurt each other for real in here." This can follow a session the previous week where you were pretty confident you had made a "breakthrough."

Interpretation of the child's affect:

Contextual cues: Child is playing out a certain theme or had indicated a different developmental stage, etc. and suddenly stops, asks to be nurtured, spaces out, regresses, suddenly asks to play Candy Land, or drink from a bottle.

Baby dolls are often used at this point in one way or another to show hurt that occurred in a pre-verbal stage.

Bodily cues: Sudden temper outburst, rigidity, listlessness, sudden disinterest in the play, sudden headache, stomach ache, reaching for a baby bottle, pacifier. Sometimes children will start crawling to indicate that stage of development or they will lay on their backs and kick their feet like an infant in a crib. These clues to the developmental stage in which they are working can be very brief. Pay attention to the bodily cues.

Flow cues: All of the above. Repetitive, circular play, getting stuck, different name or gender, sudden need to sleep- "I'm tired." "What do we play now?"

The child looks at a toy they certainly know. "What's this for?"

Therapist cues: Suddenly, you don't know your role. Are you a "good guy" or a "bad guy." Are you the Mom or the child? Confusion as to your role during reenactment play or role play is a good indicator of the child's pervasive feelings of identity confusion or inability to demonstrate a consistent core of personality traits.

Interpretation of the child's feelings or body sensations:

When body sensation, behavior, affect and knowledge are consistently consistent, dissociation is ruled out. I worked with an 11 year old boy I will call Stephen who was brought to therapy for anger and depression. He often acted very cruel and harsh with his 8-year-old-brother. He was taking paxil for depression and was prone to fantasies in which he saw himself on a "special mission from other galaxies." Like many children today, Stephen is extremely bright and seems to "know" a lot about human beings and their relationships. But not when he came to "old stuff" and established family patterns.

Both his parents were divorced and remarried and an adopted sister was added to the mix by step-mom and dad. Dad' s expectation for results in therapy almost intimidated me! I imagine they put some pressure on Stephen. He did well in school, never hurt his little sister and appeared to have adjusted to the divorce. One of the first things he disclosed to me was a UFO sighting he had had and that it was a "secret" from his parents.

During the intake session, Stephen created a sand-tray (a first) – while I discussed therapy with his mother. The sand tray clearly showed his internal conflict (alien invasions) and the need for spiritual understanding or relief (the cross and other religious symbols in the center between the

63

aliens and space men. It was a fun challenge to interpret meaning to his very left-brain father (in an alternate intake session) who was extremely reluctant to try play therapy for his son.

I had discussed the possibility of using EMDR with him at the onset of therapy.

During his eighth session, he disclosed to me that when his is with his friends he feels like he is three years old. He further disclosed that this feeling was uncomfortable, frightening and it angered him that his brother did not have those feelings. We agreed to use EMDR in his next session.

This problems revealed a conflict in sensation. He described playing Nintendo with his friends and winning. He said "I feel joyous when I win or I act like I am joyous but inside I feel scared and upset that I won."

Stephen had trouble with actual EM and did not respond well to the "buzzy thing" (thera-tapper). We quickly discovered that he would benefit the most from hand taps. His "safe place" was another planet called "Imaginary" where he was all alone except for animals. He described a beautiful sunrise, the smell of the dew and the safety he felt even with the "evil" animals. His target included a picture of playing Nintendo with his friends, winning, and feeling the two conflicted feelings. His NC was "I am ashamed." His PC was "I'm good." His SUDS level was pretty high – about a 7 or 8 in hand measurements.

The bad feeling was colored black and filled his entire body.

After installing his safe place, I asked him to hold the picture, the feeling or sensation and the belief together while I tapped his hands. He needed about 50 hand taps to access the information and was able to tell me that right away.

After the EM, he said: "It's something I've done for eight years." I told him to ask the wisest, most gentle part of himself to tell him what he needed to know.

After about 50 more hand-taps he said: "I figured the wisest part of me is my soul, so I asked my soul to tell me. Stephen quickly remembered being about three years old and holding his new baby brother. He was so happy that he had a brother and couldn't wait for him to grow up and play with him. However, his next memory involved his brother, now two years old, pushing him into a wall. Stephen responded by pushing him back and the toddler splitting his head open on a coffee table.

The parents responded by scolding him severely and comforting the younger brother. This event established a pattern in the family of always blaming Stephen when things went wrong between the brothers. As a five or six year old child, he could not tell his parents it was an act of defense to push his baby brother. He somehow associated his anger, frustration and disappointment he felt in that incident with the happiness he had felt at three when his brother was first born.

I asked him to imagine himself as a little guy after his brother got hurt and envision himself telling his parents that he was reacting to his brothers first pushing him by defending himself. They didn't believe him. So, I had him imagine that they *did* believe him and it worked. He began to see that he was not always to blame and was not entirely to blame that day years ago. That it was his *parents misperception of the incident* that caused a misperception of his motivations.

He had been perceived as jealous and mean when in fact, he felt he was justifiable in his defense. I asked him to go inside as an 11 year old and hug the little one who pushed his brother and if he felt like it to hug the toddler brother too. He did. He went back to the original target of playing Nintendo with his friends and winning. He felt the joy and NONE of the discomfort or fear. We did a little more tidying up of familial perceptions and re-installed safe place.

Then the most remarkable thing occurred. His face relaxed, it was as if I could literally see the blood circulating through his body. He said he felt "A LOT BETTER!" and his SUDS were down to almost zero (almost hands touching).

Stephen reported that the "black" color/bad feeling was almost all gone, just a tiny bit remained. He said he didn't hate his brother and didn't like hurting him.

I congratulated him on the very good job that he did and I gave him our usual ten-minute warning: "We have ten more minutes left to play for today." He said he felt better than he had in his life and he smiled at me. The look in his eyes seemed to say: "How did you know how to do that?" Then, he immediately went over to the cash register in the play room and began making money and stuffing the cash register with money of his own making. I had to smile. Stephen was metaphorically communicating to me an almost instantaneous freedom from misperceptions of himself from the past and the acquisition of increased self-esteem (*his* creation of money in the cash register.)

I have never seen anyone change physically so fast. He literally *looked* different. The tension drained from his body and his eyes smiled and relaxed. His body language softened and the usual tightness that seemed to encase him dissolved.

Then Stephen began to play. Now, he did not usually play out his true issues. He tended to build "space stations, etc. " with legos as an effort to maintain his fantasy identity and keep me reminded of how different and special he is.

Instead, Stephen picked up a kind of scary dragon puppet and played with it for a few seconds. Then he stuffed all his money and all the money from the cash register into a combination safe that "locked." He wanted to make sure his newly discovered "richness of self," would be safe and secure.

At that point, our session time was ended. He identified three feelings on the "Feelings Chart" on the way out. "Confident, happy and mischievous." But not bad or anxious or exhausted which is how he usually felt. I told him and his father that if he could feel happy when he wins with his friends and not want to really hurt his brother we would not repeat the EMDR. If he needed to repeat it, we would.

By using play therapy and EMDR his sensations and feelings became consistent with his experiences and his true essential personality.

THE USE OF TOYS IN EXPERIENTIAL PLAY: CONSIDERATIONS

1. Developmental level
2. Ability to play
3. Structure of play
4. Fantasy elements
5. Relationship between elements

THEMES: Content

1. Aggressive
2. Family/Nurturing
3. Control/Safety
4. Exploration/Mastery
5. Interactive
6. Sexualized

OTHER ASPECTS FOR CONSIDERATION:

1. World View
2. Sense of Self
3. Range of Affect
4. Response style: Internal/External
5. Developmental level
6. Issues/Concerns
7. Therapeutic needs
8. Relationship/Interpersonal or object relations

3. ****RED FLAG ALERT: SCREEN FOR....****

MPD, memory loss, intense headaches, surprise at finding things lost, completed or accomplished or found in an odd place, time loss, extensive history of abuse, sensitivity to criticism and the young child's ability to stay with the EMDR process to its completion. (See section on Dissociative Disorder Scale).

4. USING EMDR WITH DISSOCIATIVE DISORDERED CHILDREN:

Definition: the essential feature of these disorders is a disturbance or alteration in the normally integrative functions of identity, memory or consciousness. It may be gradual or sudden.

1. A troubled childhood could be summarized as years of disordered identity integration. Identity disorders often mean that a persons customary identity is forgotten and a new identity is assumed or imposed (most severe as seen in MPD).

2. A feeling of one's own reality being lost; replaced by a feeling of unreality. Children who are abused are by the very nature of abuse depersonalized; de-personalization can be a way of manifesting dissociative disorders in childhood.

3. Even small children can incur disorders of memory when traumatic events occur. When important events are not recalled an essential part of that person no longer exists (consciously).

4. Children can dissociate when something so terrible happens that to defend against, the child will divide or split his or her awareness into two levels or streams of consciousness:

a). One stream belongs to the participant in the event.

b). Another stream belongs to the observer who has been distance from the event (ie) floating over it, sees it as happening to someone else in a rather detached manner.

c). Colin Ross, M.D. (1989) defined the dissociative aspects of MPD as "a little girl imagining that the abuse is happening to someone else. This is the core of the disorder to which all other features are secondary. The act of imagining is so intense, subjectively compelling, and adaptive, that the abused child experiences dissociate aspects of herself as other people." (p. 53).

5. DO NOT USE EMDR IF YOU GET THE FOLLOWING "RED FLAGS:"

1. - The child does not have the necessary personality (ego-strength) or family support resources to cope with the material.

2. - The child's environment - ie: home life is so crisis-orientated and overwhelming that his or her ability to cope is diminished.

3. - You, as clinician, are not comfortable with the use of EMDR for this child at this particular time.

4. - You, as clinician, suspect that dissociative disorders may be moving to the far end of the continuum for this child.

5. - A sufficient level of trust has not been established.

6. - The child's level of pain/fear appears intolerable or their tolerance for emotional pain/fear is low.

7. - Child is developmentally or chronologically too young for EMDR.

8. - Poorly attached, basic trust never developed; child is victim of repeated/multiple traumas.

9. - There are no agreed upon targets.

10. - There is no safe place and after the trust has been established attempts to "find" a safe place fail.

6. POSSIBLE ALTERNATIVE PROCEEDURES:

1. - Have established a safe play relationship with the child first, which provides a "container" for the unconscious or disowned memory.

2. - Allow the play therapy process to continue until there is a fairly integrated sense of self.

3. - Oftentimes the playroom is the only "safe place," and can be utilized and installed after the therapeutic relationship is firmly established in trust.

4. - When using EMDR child protocol, check in with child frequently, look for distortions in memory, distortions in beliefs (usually about themselves), pay attention to see if the child "leaves," during EM or gets "lost."

5. - Go slow with body scans; physical sensations can trigger another memory or event.

6. - Be more consistent and systematic, less creative and spontaneous.

7. - Use hand-taps, sounds or toy of choice before using EM to prevent premature penetration of defensive barriers from being too intensive.

8. - Expect the unexpected.

9. - The therapeutic relationship needs to be strong enough to compensate for any deficiencies in the child's innate level of trust and capacity for tolerating distress, before using EMDR and distressing targets.

10. - **Double-check safe place, it may turn out to not be a safe place. Double-check any colors chosen for "light infusion," ie: the child chooses red, (often the color associated with abuse) - ask the child to tell you "happy things/good things" associated with the color red, (or any color you feel may be "suspicious").**

7. POST TRAUMA BELIEFS CHILDREN MAY HAVE & HOLD:

(These are possible NC's)

1. - I don't exist; I shouldn't be here; I'm invisible.

2. - I am bad.

3. - I deserved it.

4. - Getting mad makes it worse; having needs makes it worse.

5. - I make Mom/Caretaker crazy.

6. - I'm not lucky, I'm a looser.

7. - It's my fault.

8.   - It (the abuse) will never stop.

9.   - I am helpless.

10. - I can't tell anyone.

One of the main reasons for working with children is early intervention, alleviation and prevention of future disorders. DO NOT use any form of therapy, particularly EMDR with childhood dissociative disorders unless you have been trained/supervised and are skilled at working with these children. Experience is the key factor for the therapist treating dissociative disorders of childhood with EMDR. EMDR will always be just a part of an overall treatment plan for these children. Clinical judgment must supercede any other criteria and if in doubt, seek supervision.

SECTION 12: Resistant/Abusive Parents or Caretakers:

The family may be, and should be, the focus of treatment. In these cases, a major corrective-relationship component is required before treating the child. Parents who are resistant to their child's treatment need to confront their own fears about what the child's treatment may reveal about their parenting in their own therapy, first or simultaneously with a different therapist concurrent with the child's therapy in order to prevent future emotional damage to the child.

Ongoing abuse in a family requires family intervention services along with therapies for all family members. Children of abusive families may become at greater risk for more abuse during treatment then when not in treatment. In order for therapy to be effective, children have to be safe first. Knowing the facts regarding the current safety of the child is primary. The child must be separated from the abusive parent(s) in order to heal.

The inner world of the child must also be a visceral part of the therapists knowledge in order to give the child the respect, time and knowledge that s/he needs in order to heal. In other words, the more a therapist knows what it *feels like to be the child, the better able you will be to help the child feel better.*

Unfortunately, this separation from the original bond (be it as it may) often leads to placement in a foster home or multiple foster placements, and *every move* further traumatizes the child.

Here is a story line I see more and more often regarding a child's history: The child is abused within its birth family. Then the child is removed from its birth family by DHS and placed in foster care where s/he is either abused, neglected or cared for. Then this child may be returned to the birth parents after a serious and seriously expensive litigious battle – or not, depending on the success or failure of the "treatment plan" for the parents.

Our judicial systems are on overload. Sometimes this determination of final decree of "Parent" can take years! Meanwhile, this child has healed from the abuse – unless the Judge has insisted on frequent visitation – which has hindered the child's ability to heal – and the child's attachment disorder deepens, altering the child's natural self, her ability to learn and express in a happy, healthy way.

Now, we have an child we diagnose as PTSD (Posttraumatic Stress Disorder, *and*

Reactive Attachment Disorder *and* maybe learning delays, speech delays, issues of identity, anger, separation anxiety from members of birth family she loved, and on and on. The more you can imagine the *feeling of a* developmental nightmare of a child, the more you can lead them to the light.

Another more frequent reason for therapy is Parent Alienation Syndrome and it behooves you as a child therapist to educate yourself on this very sad syndrome.

A. INTERPLAY OF PARENTAL ISSUES & CHILDREN'S THERAPY: A BRIEF OVERVIEW

When unhealthy parental issues are unresolved, it may seem like EMDR doesn't work with the child. In play, the themes can become circular, unnecessarily repetitive and unproductive or regressive. These can be signals that work with the parent's issues is essential either within the context of the child's therapy or alone with another therapist. It is generally best to refer the parents to a trusted adult therapist and confine your meetings with the parent to focus on the child and parenting issues.

Circular and repetitive play may suggest that a harmful person is still invading a child's environment. Know that the child's unfolding map of brain networking/chemistry is being altered in a negative way while therapy is struggling to correct it. I tell parents at this point that the therapy is "maintenance." The play with or without EMDR will help the child to catch up as much as possible developmentally, support the child and strengthen the child but will not necessarily reach its most optimum conclusion.

The time-honored controversy regarding the interplay between Nature Vs. Nurture concept of human development really becomes complex when *so many disruptions to normal development have occurred for the child in addition to parental diagnosis.*

What I have observed from playing with hundreds of children and their caretakers is that the child is like the "hardware," of a computer (the vessel of expression of the essential self). The child's basic "personality and temperment," are the natural outpouring of a "hard drive program" springing from soul and spirit" – genetically and spiritually constructed to live life as a certain human being. Depending on the "software" (the environmental influence, nurturing, bonding, etc) installed into the "hard drive" and how the "hardware" and the "software" interface – behaviors, beliefs and the child's literal programming becomes a part of the computer. Unfortunately, abusive parents install too much contaminated "software" into a new computer (the child) and a virus called "trauma" replaces the anti-virus called "love." Uninstalling negative programming and nasty viruses is difficult and it is best for the clinician to feel the child's difficulty, respect the child, let go and let life and do good work.

Considerations for assessment:

1. Child's developmental level
2. Child's functional level or adaptive level
3. Developmental changes
4. Prior circumstances
5. Family type/Social Class
6. Psychosocial stressors
7. Physical health
8. Intensity, Frequency & Duration
9. Parent/Child Interaction
10. Birth Order/Size of Family

Family Patterns: (Causality not clear - general impressions).

1. ADHD/ADD - Increased depression in mothers/increased marital discord. Often disorganized home and feelings of failure, low self esteem.

2. CONDUCT/OPPOSTIONAL DISORDERS -Antisocial behavior transmitted across generations: Genetic & Environmental Factors

*Parents are more likely to suffer from various psychiatric disorders, criminal behavior and alcoholism.

* Aggressive behavior traced across generations.

*Divorce, harsh discipline

3. ANXIETY DISORDERS - 91% of these children's mothers have anxiety disorders: 64% current. 11% of mothers had avoidant disorder.

4. PHOBIC DISORDERS - (Not conclusive)

*Overindulgent mother/passive father

*Over controlled mother/passive father

*Overindulgent mother/firm father

19% of parents had separation anxiety

*Agoraphobic mothers

5. OCD -

* As little as 1% to 21% in parental/sibling diagnosis

* Higher than normal incidence for psychiatric disorders in relatives, OCD in particular.

* Family role unclear

6. SCHIZOID DISORDERS -

* Disorder constitutional in nature and in family patterns

* Family role unclear

7. AUTISM -

* Family role unclear

8. SCHIZOPHRENIA-

* Dominant gene

* More common in second-degree relatives

* Family role unclear.

9. BI-POLAR -

* Genetic transmission

* 20% of parent diagnosis

* 85% - 1 relative with bipolar illness

10. MAJOR DEPRESSION -

* Children with depression come from the most heavily "affectively loaded" families.

* Child risk increased with parental major depression

* Morbid risk for alcoholism and anxiety disorders

11. FUNCTIONAL EURESIS & ENCOPRESIS-

*75% of first-degree relatives of enuresis have also been enuretic

* Stronger for males than females

* (Encopresis) - little known; 15% of fathers

12. FIRE SETTING & PYROMANIA-

* Parental depression, past and current mental disorders, greater range of parental psychiatric symptoms

* History of parental fire setting/arson - undetermined.

("Annual Progress In Child Psychiatry & Child Development," Hertzog & Farber, 1996).

This list is by no means meant to be conclusive or comprehensive. It is a general list to review to get a *feel* for patterns of the interplay between parental psychopatholgy and the child's therapy.

In experiential play therapy a child will attempt to show a parent's pathology for example, by playing in the kitchen and making a meal and hen suddenly running over and putting on a scary alien mask and "switching" into a very frightening monster who yells at the child (you). n the working stages of therapy it is your job to let the child know that you know what it feels like to be suddenly attacked by a parent who is "nice" one minute and "mean" the next.

I once had a child who kept a very scary wolf man mask on while we had tea. This child's fear had become so common place it was literally "at home" and a part of his nurturing experience.

Less pervasive issues or issues not defined as psychopathology per se, such as divorce, gender identity disorders of parents, religion, promiscuity, adultery, trans-gendered parents, gay and lesbian parents, alcoholism, substance abuse, critical, absent, unresolved sexual abuse or other abuse, MPD, poor limit-setting, diffuse boundaries, secondary gains, etc. all affect the child's treatment to a greater or lesser degree. The parent's trust in the clinician, the X's objection to you as a clinician, the parent's perception of therapy in general, court-ordered vs. self-referred children, adoption. This list is potentially never-ending.

The main responsibility is to assess how the parental issues will inhibit or enhance the child's therapy using either/or EMDR or PLAY and to include those variables in your clinical decisions when working with a child.

An on-going dialogue between parent/therapist is the best form of communication. As a more trusting relationship develops over time with the parents, you, the clinician have, not only support and cooperation but access to more information about the child and parental disclosure. Family of origin issues and marital issues frequently emerge during these dialogues and areas of unresolved issues that can *substantially (qualitatively and quantitatively) effect their child's treatment.* These are important considerations for recommending parental/family therapy or other form of adjunct treatment.

It also will give you more insight into the meaning of the child's metaphors in both experiential play and EMDR.

Most parents are open to talking with you, their child's therapist themselves *when it is limited to parenting issues.* It is important to know how parents set limits and how they react to their child's behavior. "How do you discipline your child?"

You may recommend EMDR therapy to help desensitize parents reactivity to their child's behaviors and help develop a more appropriate and healthy parental response. This raises everyone's self-esteem, dignity and sets up a more positive cycle of interaction.

B. EMDR & COURT:

"Clients who must give a detailed account of the incident to the police or in court must be warned that after (EMDR) treatment a picture of the event may not be retrievable. Some clients become confused or disturbed when the picture begins to disappear." (EMDR, Basic Principals. Protocols and Procedures, Francine Shapiro, p.82).

"..... in many courts the use of hypnosis in any phase of a client's treatment can contaminate his ability to take legal action against the perpetrator. EMDR is clinically very dissimilar to hypnosis, and recent EEG studies indicate that the brain waves produced during EMDR treatment and those produced during hypnosis are quite different from each other..... In addition, in a recent court case involving alleged sexual abuse the judge ruled that EMDR was not akin to hypnosis and could not implant false memories.....However, EMDR may face more legal challenges in the future. Consequently, the clinician should inform the client of the possible legal issues before EMDR treatment is commenced. However, refraining from using hypnosis along with EMDR may make the case more forensically tenable." (Ibid., p. 293.)

A basic rule of thumb for EMDR and court is this: if the child must go to court and remember the bad feelings and events in order to prosecute an abuser, EMDR may erase the bad feelings and memories associated with the perpetrator. Clinical judgment is called for when deciding "how long" should a clinician wait to give the child relief. Keeping children out of court is best; however, other agencies may be called in to investigate or question the child. Please discuss the possible implications with parents when making this crucial decision. Play therapy can always be offered until such interrogations are complete. It is a hard decision to make - consult with other professionals too when investigations are involved in a case.

EMDR does a lot better in court than experiential play therapy. NEVER try to use the play of a child to support allegations of any

kind of child abuse. Our system is not yet advance enough or educated enough in early childhood development to accept a child's play as evidence of abuse. If you suspect that abuse has actually occurred, try and get the child to verbalize his or her story at least one time before making a report. Then you can use play themes to back up the verbalization. If you have an attorney, run the evidence you have by your attorney prior to making your report. Because we operate under a mandatory reporting law, a suspicion of child abuse must be reported.

But be careful not to be 100% certain of who the abuser is in your report (even if you know in your gut) as to who committed the alleged abuse especially if you feel confident reporting from only a child's play themes. We are not investigators; we are healers. In our current system, you will benefit the child much more by remembering your role and keeping it pure.

I was involved in two separate cases where two six-year-old girls *told me verbally* of their natural father's sexual abuse toward them. I dutifully reported. Three years later, one case is still "under investigation" because the fathers' (both fathers) attorney filed a claim against me saying I needed to be "stopped."

He further assured the Regulatory Board that he was not conducting a "witch hunt" against me. He likes to defend perpetrators and he used to defend drunk drivers. Beware of attorney pathology, agency and other therapist pathology too. But that's the subject of another book. Stick to your role as facilitator for the child's best healing opportunity at the time you have the child on your caseload.

SECTION 13: More creative ways to process body sensations/NC's, PC's:

1. SANDTRAY/SAND PLAY: Themes, feelings & pictures

A). Making the unconscious conscious:

1). Messages In Sand Tray/Play

a) Common Themes

War: Internal Conflict - Good vs. Bad

External Conflict - Divorce

Disability/Empowerment

Good/Evil

Safety/Protection

Self-esteem

Secrets/Hidden

Hero/Villain

Power/Powerlessness

Aggressive/Passive

Scary/Comforting

Abandonment

Betrayal

Rescue, etc.

b) Uses/Symbolic Meaning of Sand

Reflection of child's emotional state/psyche

Construction/Destruction

Environment

Community

Feelings/Emotions

Change

Creativity

Regression

Covert/Hidden

Unacknowledged

Express/Withdraw

Intense/Light

Deep/Surface

Pressure/Relief

Full/Hollow-Empty

Separation Issues

Death/loss

c)   Therapeutic Issues

Who I am/My mind

Organization/disorganization

Termination

Suicidal Ideation

Core Issues

Diagnostic Issues

Perfection

Control/Chaos

Predictable/Unpredictable

Scarcity/Abundance

Who, what etc., does the child identify with? This is the child's present state of mind. Who, what etc., would be better for the child to identify with represents the goal.

2. SAND TRAY/SAND PLAY USES WITH EMDR:

Pictures, externalization of feelings, dramatization of situations, events, conflicts, etc. can all be used to select targets for EMDR processing. The earlier example, of using sand play and play-dough and integrating EMDR processing gives the clinician an idea of how to use this concept.

In Play therapy, sand is considered an essential medium for expression.

THE SAND:

Three dimensional/tactile

Soothing – white, soft, clean

Fluid/grounding

Used as rain, snow, mud and dirt

Dry Sand: Usually a child's first choice

Wet Sand: Used for construction in the 0-5 age range is appropriate. Excessive water play in older children can demonstrate weak ego development, inability to comprehend limits and reality. Can be indicative of aggressive impulses.

Mixing Wet & Dry Sand: Children who mix dry and wet sand often exhibit a lack of impulse control. Children can also have a definite purpose in mind...but should be able to provide a rational explanation for behavior. ("The Erica Method," A Technique for Play Therapy and Diagnosis: A Training Guide, Margareta Sjolund,Ph.D).

Understanding "normal" or undisrupted childhood development is very important in using sand tray material for assessment since the same play can have completely different meanings at different stages of development. A two-year old who "dumps" toys in the sand has a different meaning than a five-year old who "dumps" toys in the sand.

3. USING SAND TO ASSESS THE EMOTIONAL STABILITY OF YOUR CLIENT:

Play Observations:

Avoidance or use of sand

Touching with hands or tool

Regressive play

Marking hand/foot prints - Identity/anxiety

Hiding - Secrets, object constancy/self - object identified

With

Loss of self esteem/possible indication of abuse

Hiding/Finding - Separation anxiety

Burying/ Secrets/Wishes/Death/Trauma

Placement: Meaningful/Indifferent

Categorizing: Developmental Skill/Defense

Relationship between toys

Ability to create "meaningful scenes"

Dumping toys randomly

Bizarre groupings

Fences, walls

(Ibid)

During processing, focus on the object - focus on the feeling. Use the "I wonder?" question. "I wonder what it would feel like to live in that place?" or "What kind of animal do you need/want to be?" Or "for me to be?"

When a sand tray has been constructed by a child the clinician can comment on the object in the sand or ask for a "story." I ask questions, within the safety of the child's created metaphor to process and to find targets for EMDR. A child creates a "town" or a "place" in the sand. I would say, "If you were pretending to be someone in that town, which one would it be?" or "I wonder what it's like for that one (pointing to an object) to live in that town."

Keeping your questions confined to the objects in the sand tray will elicit story telling from your young client. I say: "Tell me the story of your picture." Then I take two Polaroid photos, one for them and one for me. "Your job is to give the story a title. What title should I write on this for you?" Child generated titles for sand trays often summarize the essence of the experience they are relating.

SECTION 14: The Anxious Child:

POSSIBLE SYMPTOMS:

1. Unrealistic worry: about major attachment figures, catastrophic harm, abandonment, kidnapping, murder, etc. These symptoms may occur more frequently as incidents such as Littleton, CO. increase in frequency.

2. Persistent refusal to go to school, be away from major attachment

3. figure, impact of societal violence on the child,

4. Avoidance of being alone, upset when can't follow major attachment figure around the house,

5. Reluctance to sleep alone, away from home, nightmares involving separation/loss themes

6. Physical complaints on school days

7. Excessive separation distress

8. Social withdrawal/apathy, sadness, lack of concentration

9. Preoccupation with appropriateness of behavior in the past

10. Excessive need for reassurance

11. Extreme self-consciousness, susceptibility to humiliation

12. Marked feelings of tension - inability to relax.

13. Self-harming behaviors

There are, of course, different disorders of anxiety and EMDR treats different anxiety disorders specifically. EMDR processes present and past memories and in children. It seems to be best to go backward from present to the past and (future/anticipatory anxiety).

Most anxiety disorder symptoms are caused by a disturbing event and/or living with an anxious parent. The anxiety can become linked to a number of things: sights, sounds, mother's voice, certain places, etc. The web of anxiety can be complex, even in childhood but the positive treatment effects can spread throughout the child's memory networking system on a lot of levels very quickly. Often, when a state of relaxation is experienced it can be installed over time. I've used "meditation" tapes of a simple visualization variety with older, anxious children. After the meditation, I install the feeling of relaxation and the soothing visualization right after we "come back" to the playroom. Over time, the ability to self-soothe and self-regulate will be internalized by the child. We also work to find the "triggers" to signal the need for self-soothing.

Because EMDR is considered a "breakthrough therapy," for treating anxiety, stress and trauma, both EMDR and play therapy will serve an anxious young client and help them to overcome their anxiety, often at the source. Most anxiety begins with a disturbing experience and because of the linked memory system which is so richly and advantageously used during EMDR, the genesis of many sources of anxiety can be eliminated.

Association and classical conditioning are very basic psychological processes and children are prone to make quick connections that are "Pavolvian" and associative.

Some of the most recent research in the treatment of childhood anxiety and EMDR "...showed that subjects who did eye movements while thinking about their disturbing memory seemed to have an automatic physical relaxation response. .... the results of this study also underline how powerful the link is between our physiology and our psychology. .... after a single session of EMDR, the subject's primary symptoms disappeared."

(EMDR, The Breakthrough Therapy for Overcoming Anxiety, Stress and Trauma, Shapiro & Forrest, p. 68.)

Why then, if EMDR is so effective in treating anxiety, should we bother with play therapy?

In Joseph Chilton Pearce's book, Evolutions End, he asserts the following regarding playing and childhood: "Play develops intelligence, integrates our triune nature; prepares us for higher education, creative thought, and taking part in and upholding a social structure; and helps us prepare for becoming an effective parent when the time comes. Play is the very force of society and civilization and a breakdown in ability to play will reflect in a breakdown of society. We are a tough, resilient species; our capacity to compensate for damage is enormous.... (Harper San Francisco, 1993). (He then continues a scathing evaluation of the effects of television, day care abandonment and electronics and the neurological damage it does to our children.)

Play is the natural expression of the child. If a parent wants to improve their relationship *immediately* with their child they should play with them. Children learn almost everything through play.

Play is a good way to form a relationship with an anxious child, particularly because children, plain and simple, like and need to play. Children are rarely experiencing high levels of anxiety while playing and when they do experience anxiety in their play, the means of self-expression and release are available to them. Play therapy also offers a more holistic and integrative level of incorporating new information on the experiential level. It gives children a chance to be creative in processing on a deeply physical level and also offers a range of styles in which to do this.

It is difficult for children, if not impossible for some, to verbalize their feelings. Most kids do not understand their feelings, especially young children. Play allows the recreation of the experiences that cause anger, fear, sadness, frustration and rage. EMDR also allows for the recreation or remembering of the same experiences which can be re-processed within the complex workings of the brain. But for children, the immediate physical resolution or "follow-through," with the re-processed information seals that within their being and becomes a *total holistic experience. And in pre-pubescent children appears to be a strong contributing factor to altering a child's brain chemistry in a positive way.*

This total holistic experience anchors the feeling of mastery and control over situations in the way that children truly understand them - *through their play.* The integration of Play and EMDR is so complete and powerful because by their very natures EMDR and Play are as complimentary as two puzzle pieces.

Play therapy is often a "dress rehearsal" for life. (Norton) Therapeutic play provides both cognitive and emotional development as well as the integration of motor development. The ability to develop an internal world rich with symbolic meaning, imagination and creativity stems from play in infancy and the quality of play throughout childhood. Experiential play therapy enhances the gains made by EMDR and EMDR enhances the gains of Play.

THE PLAY OF THE ANXIOUS CHILD:

Can range from no activity, exploring with the eyes only, hand twisting with the child being "at a loss" as to what to do in the playroom at first to over-active play that might mimic ADHD behavior. Because the anxious child's main motivation is to gain adult approval they will either wait and see what you want, ask a lot of questions, or be so nervous they will not be able to focus on the toys in a meaningful way. The child will be afraid to take risks at first until the absolute safety of the playroom eases her anxiety. The playroom experience is a good place for the child to experience the anxiety and learn to take the emotional risks necessary in order to overcome it.

Children who suffer from separation anxiety will be very concerned or even unable to leave parents to come into the playroom with you, the therapist. In this case, regardless of the age of the child, she should be accompanied by the parent into the playroom. However, it is very important to keep the main focus on the child and not the parent. The parent needs to be quiet and the interaction between the parent and child should be kept to a minimum to allow the child the opportunity to take some small risks. One goal of the therapy becomes helping the child eventually reduce her anxiety enough in order to enter the playroom without the parent. Most children over four years old will come into the playroom with the therapist even for the first session.

Sometimes the anxious child with separation anxiety will transfer their need for an adult figure onto the therapist and will resist separating from you, the toys and the playroom. I have found that giving a longer warning for ending the session helps these children. At the 15 minute mark, I may say, "We have 10 more minutes left to play for today." Then at the 10 minute mark, I would say, "We have 5 minutes left to play for today, then we will clean up, get a treat and say good-bye to the toys for today." This way the anxious child has time to adjust to the idea of change and is not hurried out of the playroom.

1. SINGLE vs. MULTIPLE TRAUMA: Considerations

1). The developmental stage of the child when the trauma(s) happened.

2). The age of the child at the onset of the trauma.

3). The level of resolution following the trauma.

For some children, single traumas can have just as devastating effect as multiple- trauma. However, if we measure the effects of trauma by intensity, frequency and duration - it is clear that the more trauma/abuse experienced, the more deeply rooted or imprinted the negative beliefs become in the child's mind, being, psyche, and soul.

Both Play therapy and EMDR can help establish a sense of well-being and balance over time for both single and multiple trauma victims. The most important factor in healing is the point of current resolution which then gives hope and a goal for resolution. The clinician needs to be most aware of trauma that has not stopped and take the appropriate clinical actions.

NOTE: Children can and do resist EMDR processing by claiming to have his or her "happy" feeling really bigger prematurely. They are smart enough to know what you want to hear. This does not happen very often but it can happen. However, my experience with these few children who are clever enough or too frightened to process traumatic events using EMDR is that just using the EMDR process will <u>move the play along if the play has become "stuck" for the same reasons.</u> For example, a 5 year-old child who was a victim of on-going, ritualistic, day-care abuse believed his family would be killed if he "told." He was very cautious (or blocked) even in his play for longer than usual and for his own good reasons. When he realized the power of EMDR to elicit information - he created the "dance of resistance" to keep me from learning about the abuse. I had to let him know that I already knew about the abuse for a long time and that nothing bad had happened to him or his family.

He danced around the EMDR process with even more "fancy footwork," but even a few sets of hand taps got his play moving again right away. The handtaps grounded him. He was able to bring his "whole body" back into the playroom and put aside his very strong tendency to intellectualize and dissociate from his traumas.

THE PLAY OF SINGLE VS. MULTIPLE TRAUMA CHILDREN:

Children who have experienced a single trauma or acute trauma that is not chronic or ongoing will be able to utilize the therapeutic relationship quickly in order to heal that trauma. Although they usually present as an anxious child, their trust level of you and the process is more intact. They will respond much more quickly to therapy and this is particularly true when combining the play therapy with EMDR. A child with chronic trauma or multiple traumas will spend a lot more time trying to establish a trusting relationship with you. Children with a single trauma, in general, have trusting relationships with adults. Children with multiple traumas will be testing you often, exhibit depressive/angry features and is used to feeling traumatized.

In other words, the single-trauma child will usually show you what they were like prior to the trauma while the child with multiple or chronic trauma has internalized stress as a "normal" feeling for them. The child with multiple trauma has most likely already experienced a change in their style of play.

They will not generally go back and show you life before the traumatic events although they may communicate a wish to be "a baby again." That might have been the last time they felt safe or that life (themselves) was good. For the multiple trauma child, dysfunctional patterns for play and life are already set in motion. For the single or acute trauma child, they are not.

2. STAGE FOUR (Norton's Experiential Model) Utilization of EMDR in the Therapeutic Growth Stage:

After the intense working stages of therapy using both EMDR and play, more positive things start to happen in the playroom and in the child's life. The child's play will become less intense and more normalized play will take up therapy time. Therapeutic growth is a time when the child can experience the well-deserved feeling of competency and power that they have earned. This is a true reclaiming of the essence of their being, of themselves. It is a stage of transformation where the child can regain the benefits of the developmental stages that were missed and grow. In experiential play, the child will combine the working stages and therapeutic growth until the play session becomes neutral, positive, empowering.

The therapist verbally reinforces all the positive growth during this stage of therapy. "Remember when you first came into the playroom, how scary it all seemed? And how you had trouble _____? Now you can_____ and it isn't scary at all. Now you can do a lot of things you couldn't do before." or "Now you have friends that are nice to you," or "The divorce was hard on you, now you can accept that you have two homes even though it's still sad sometimes."

These positive statements can be reinforced by EM and further installed that way. The child's safe place or self image has probably changed by this stage of play therapy. Check to see what positive beliefs the child now has about herself and install them. Install the feeling of success and self-knowledge based on the child's own experience of herself separate from the trauma.

Goal: Re claiming positive/true identity and dignity.

A child who I will call Sam, upon entering Stage Four of Play - or therapeutic growth - created a wonderful and powerful metaphor to signal his transition and transformation out of the intense parts of the working stages of play.

Sam, a 6 year old, came from a supportive, intact family. However, because his father was in the military, he was gone for long periods of time. His mother became a virtual "single-parent" with younger twins to care for as well as Sam.

His abuse occurred in a day-care setting with a day-care provider he had loved and trusted for over two years. After the day care provider married a certain man, she changed. She and her new husband began sexually abusing Sam. His sense of fear, anger and betrayal were enormous particularly because a loved and trusted adult had betrayed him so deeply.

One day, Sam entered the playroom and busily constructed a complex "generator," (his word) out of a variety of building materials in the playroom. This "generator" changed "gas" into "energy" by traveling through a series of tubes and connectors. This was Sam's way of telling me that his energy was transforming. He was beginning to embrace the fact that the abuse was not his fault and heal the deep hurt he had experience over this horrific betrayal of his trust. He was very happy and excited during this session.

His mother was observing his session that day. Her eyes met mine when Sam and I left the playroom. "He's getting better," she said to me. I could read the relief and gratitude in her face.

During the following session, Sam constructed a car and invited me to go on a trip with him. He filled the car with nurturing toys, toys of safety and protection and he was in control as the driver. Sam created a "map" – a feeling of new direction – one which the "bad guys" couldn't read. In fact, our car left them in the dust. He was headed literally in a "new direction," able to see himself as separate from the abuse he endured.

Utilizing EMDR in the Therapeutic Growth stage is relatively simple and pleasurable for both the client and the clinician. The safe place may have changed; new goals and more positive images of self may emerge. Different insights or perspectives on past traumatic events will surface and positive beliefs should be installed. This is a very rewarding stage of therapy for everyone. Finally, all the work/play that the child has generated with the support of their family and you start to take root and grow. The rewards go very deep. At this point, there is generally little to no resistance to using EMDR to reinforce the gains of play or EMDR sessions.

Sometime with severely traumatized children, I will wait until this stage of play to integrate EMDR and use only safe place and positive installations to reinforce the play therapy experience or to make sure the channels associated with the trauma are cleared out.

NOTE OF CAUTION: As clinician, you must be very careful not to resurrect trauma that has been resolved in the play thus re-traumatizing the child. Usually if I have waited to integrate EMDR until therapeutic growth stage, I have done so to protect the child and limit the use of EMDR to safe place and positive installations. With EMDR you can never be 100% sure that nothing traumatic will resurface although it is now my experience that when the trauma is truly resolved, it will not resurface in an upsetting way.

SECTION 15: Taking a break from EMDR & Play!

Using child/parent/therapist generated narratives to help heal (and find targets for processing):

Concept: To parallel the child's experience as closely as possible using (usually) animals as metaphors in the story instead of people - again to protect the child's ego. Other children can be used in the parallel narrative as well as toys in the playroom that a child has identified with over and over again to tell their story in play.

Stories provide some distance and displacement from sensitive issues as do other forms of play therapy. Children like and need to identify with the characters as it creates a sense of "this happens to other kids," and decreases feelings of extreme isolation.

Modeled after the basic ingredients for fairly tales, the leading role in the therapeutic narrative involves a villain or conflict to overcome. Varieties of adaptive roles and attitudes for conflict resolution can be transferred to the child through stories.

"Each story contains a metaphorical conflict, unconscious strengths and potentials, parallel learning situations, a metaphorical crisis, a new identification for the protagonist, and ends in a celebration of the characters. (Creating Metaphors for Children and the Child Within, Drs. Mills & Crowley, 1986)."

Stories used for EMDR or in play sessions need to include the child (the protagonist) pre-trauma level of functioning, strengths and situation.

The child's therapeutic issues are woven into the story and are used by the parent, foster parent, or therapist to help the child. Stories help soften bad news and are used as a "bridge technique," that involves telling the story, then introducing new information with the phrase, "Just like the character in the story ....."

The telling of the story involves, relaxation, imagination, sensory descriptions, visual, auditory and kinesthetic aspects, toys, voice/tone inflection/intonation and facial expressions. (Therapeutic Stories for Children in Foster Care, Karen Lanners & Ken Schwartzenberger).

Telling stories over and over has a desensitizing effect on children as well as providing validation, comfort and physical closeness. Besides, story-telling helps the child to exercise their imaginative powers so necessary later in life for problem solving.

Parent-generated stories provide clear examples of or clues to parental issues that may be influencing the child's progress in therapy.

I read this story to "J" during the termination stage of therapy and it really helped to put closure on her six months worth of play-work in therapy. Since her trauma occurred between 9 months and 18 months of age and her experience of play therapy occurred at 6 years, I felt she needed extra grounding and closure during Therapeutic Growth and Termination.

A. J's story in play "translated" by her therapist V. McGuinness

This is a story about a very cute, very small koala bear. It wasn't just that her Mom thought that she was cute. Everyone thought so! This koala bear was fury and soft. This very small bear went to play at another Big Animal's den during the day while her Moma and Popa Koala went to work. Most mornings, Moma Bear would take her little cute Koala bear to Ms. Bat's den. Ms. Bat took care of little bears and other animals while their parent's worked during the day. Ms. Bat had two helpers; they were snakes. One was green and one was blue. One snake was Ms. Bat's husband - he was green, and the other snake, was her son - he was blue. Moma Bear and little Koala thought that Ms. Bat and her snake helpers seemed pretty nice. So, Moma Bear left little Koala in Ms. Bat's den with her bottle and her blankey while she went to work.

Ms. Bat cared for a lot of baby cubs and other animals; little Koala trusted her and the snakes for a long time. It seemed that she was being taken good care of, even though little Koala really missed her Mom. Then one day, one of the tiny, white mice babies were tricked and given something bad to eat by Ms. Bat. At first, it tasted good, but then the tiny white mice babies got really sick from eating it. Little Koala watched the whole thing; but she couldn't tell anyone because she was too small to talk! Poor Koala! Poor baby mice! They all had tummy aches.

Oh! Little Koala wanted to know: "Where is my Mom??" "Where is my Dad?" "Why don't they come and take me home!!!" "I'm so scared!" One baby mouse got so sick that he had to go to the hospital. He never came back. Little Koala just knew he had died!!! She was so scared that in the morning when her Moma dropped her off at Ms. Bat's house she would holler and scream to warn her mother in the only way she could.

But Ms. Bat told Moma Bear that all was well and so, little Koala was left there anyway. Ms. Bat lied and told Moma Bear that little Koala stopped crying right after she drove away.

One day, Ms. Bat called Moma Bear up at work and said that Little Koala bear had hurt her head and had a big bump on it because of an accident. A few days later, Moma Bear decided to take her little Koala somewhere else to play. She took her baby bear to Ms. Lamb's house. Ms. Lamb was really nice, but Little Koala was so afraid that she would get hurt or that some other little animal would get hurt that she cried and screamed so fearfully that Ms. Lamb said that Little Koala would have to go play somewhere else.

Two more times Moma Koala brought her baby to new Big Animal's dens to play but Little Koala just knew someone would trick her and the other small animals so she fought and kicked and bit to protect herself and the others. Now, there was nowhere for Little Koala to be safe during the day while her parents worked. Little Koala had turned "mean." Little Koala felt mean, too, but deep down inside she knew she was nice! And so did Moma & Papa Koala Bear. Little Koala was so mixed-up inside.

Poor Little Koala! She didn't know if she was a good bear or a bad bear! When Little Koala had her three-year old birthday, Moma Koala took her to a safe place to play during the day when her parents worked. By now, Little Koala could say a lot of bear words and Moma Koala knew she would tell if any big animal was hurting her or scaring her. Little Koala was safe for a long time. Then after Little Koala had her five-year old birthday part, Moma Koala said: "Now! It's time for Kindergarten! *Real bear school! You are not a baby bear anymore!"* Little Koala was so excited about going to <u>real school!</u> All the bad things that happened to her as a baby bear were all forgotten about. But when Little Koala got to the big bear real school something bad happened. She started biting her claws and scratching the other school animals, she hit them and hurt them. She called them names. She had to! If she didn't keep them away from her they would get hurt. The worst part was, Little Koala could not tell anyone why she acted this way. Her Moma and Popa became very worried about her.

No one, not even her teachers could understand why she acted this way.

Then one day, Moma Koala took Little Koala to see a Big Play Animal who loved to play with her in any way that she wanted. Little Koala loved the play room with so many toys! She felt safe in that room and with the Big Play Animal. They played and played for a long time. The Big Play Animal laughed at Koala who wanted other animals to know she was funny. The Big Play Animal kept showing Little Koala what a fine little bear she really was and gave her new ideas about herself. One day, they met in a deep, dark cave where Little Koala was lost. The Big Play Animal found her and helped her find a way out of the deep, dark, cold cave where Little Koala had been lost for a long time - all by herself!

After Little Koala and the Big Play Animal left the cave, hand-in-hand, they entered the light. There before them lay a soft, green meadow enclosed by a strong, black fence. A gate opened into the mysterious forest where birds sang and squirrels screeched. Little Koala felt a mixture of courage and challenge.

Little Koala armed herself with a gun, and stationed the Big Play Animal in their camp. They communicated by walkie-talkie. Little Koala hunted for wolves and mean Bears. She was a little bit frightened. Many creatures lived in the forest and Little Koala had not met them yet. She imagined what they would be like. But she told herself she would return to the peaceful meadow after the bad guys were punished, killed and gone forever.

There were a lot of close calls for Little Koala and the Big Play Animal (BPA) before the mean ones were chased away, captured or killed. Little Koala noticed that she didn't feel so scared anymore. A new feeling was filling her up. She felt brave and kind. She knew she was! She could protect herself and other small animals when they wanted to play with her before she had gotten so mean. "I'm not mean; I'm happy!" Little Koala said to herself. She marched up to the Big Play Animal and said as she dropped her armor and gun, "Let's go camping in the meadow."

"You got all the bad ones?"

"Yes, I did," and Little Koala sat down to rest.

"You are a happy bear now that you know the truth about yourself. You are good and brave, funny and smart. Let's go camping in the meadow. You got the bad guys and we can just play now."

While they were camping, Little Koala thought about her adventures. 'Am I a hero?" she asked the BPA. "What do you think?" the BPA asked back. "Yes," replied Koala realizing as she said it that she was almost coming up to her six-year old birthday party.... and that meant.... she really was not a baby anymore!!!

She loved the BPA when BPA looked at her and agreed: "Yes, you are a hero, Koala. You are so right."

When little Koala went back to the big, real bear school she quickly showed everyone that she was happier and stronger. Her friends were so happy to play with her! Her teacher was thrilled to see Little Koala be happy and pretty in her dresses... and smart to. Moma and Popa Koala relaxed. They decided to go to Disney Land on a great big boat.

But Little Koala had one more little adventure to go on before she could leave with her family for Disney Land. One day, she found a little dalmation puppy. She immediately named the puppy, "Two-tone." After examining him, she knew he had been poisoned a long time ago and that he was dying. She brought Two-tone to see the BPA and they performed a long, difficult operation. They prayed that they got all the poison out. They wrapped Two-tone's tummy with a special white bandage and snuggled Two-tone into Koala's bed. Koala watched over Two-tone all week. He was so cute! He was the best puppy Koala had ever had. She just kept on believing that the operation had worked.

The next week, BPA and Koala unwrapped Two-tone's bandage. It was true! Two-tone was better! Two-tone was healing from an old, old injury that no one could ever see. Pretty soon after that, Koala and BPA were saying "Good-Bye." Now Koala had friends at school and everyone said how much happier everyone was. Koala and her family were leaving for Disney Land. Koala was six years old. She was taking Two-tone with her everywhere; for now, they were the best of friends.

Whenever Koala or Two-tone thought about bad guys or mean animals, they said to each other: "We got 'em before. Even if sometimes they're scary. If they try to scare us again, we'll get 'em again."

FIN

In the interest of time, I have learned to tell summarizing stories spontaneously and perhaps with more brevity. This technique honors the child's experience and reflects back to the child her ability to change her internalized beliefs about herself. Very empowering for the child.

SECTION 16: Creating Meaningful Metaphors in Personalized Story-Form

A child's troubled behavior in and out of the playroom is often a distinctive metaphor within itself. It is a message to adults in the child's world that the relationship that the child is experiencing with the world around her is too overwhelming for her to handle alone. The following is a viewing of "J's" play, the metaphors she created and my role as therapist to recognize and utilize her themes to her benefit. Not knowing what else to do, "J" uses a form of protection that seems right to her - to kick and scratch and bit and yell to keep everyone away.

Children rarely, if ever say to themselves: "I'm scared of something I witnessed/experienced when I was a baby. So now, I will need to protect myself and all the other kids by keeping everyone away from me. If other kids come near me, they'll get hurt and so will I. I have to be meaner and stronger than everyone to stay safe; but then, no one likes me."

She is caught in the classic Metaphorical Conflict that has emerged out of the original conflict of being left in a covertly abusive environment at a pre-verbal stage of development. From the time she was in an abusive day-care situation, even from 9 mos. of age to 18 mos. of age, she was fully able to record and experience acts of maltreatment and abuse that she witnessed (as secondary victim) or experienced (as primary victim). She must protect herself and others by being "mean," and in the process she is sacrificed. She feels all alone.

During the process of play, she discovers her Unconscious Strengths and Potentials. This is the classic format of fairly tales. "J" discovers that she tried as hard as she could when she was just a baby to communicate her danger to her mother. She also learned that she cared so much for others, that she was willing to sacrifice her life for them. "J" learned that she could always survive and always be cared for.

To create meaningful metaphors a Parallel Learning Situation needs to exist. As "J" confronts her fears about the world and herself, she is "found" by a Big Play Animal who cares about her. They emerge from the dark cave together and into the meadow. Her fears subside. She rests and reflects. But challenges await her. "J" has to become heroic to confront the effects and consequences of her traumas. She arms herself (with new defenses that are more healthy and effective) and "gets the bad guys." She can now rest and celebrate. As she explores her inner emotional resources in order to find out that she is truly good, she becomes courageous and brave. " "J" has found a New Identification as she slays the enemy within herself. She remembers to heal the "inner baby" part of herself, which she creates in the character and friend of "Two-tone."

The completion of the metaphor culminates in Celebration. But in "J's" case, before we can celebrate, another heroic action is called for. She "finds" Two-tone. Perhaps she is remembering the "baby" victim that was herself. He is poisoned. Poison is a very complete metaphor for the contamination of her being that the disreputable day care providers caused to "J's" being.

During the middle phase of treatment, during the Working Stage of therapy, DHS was contacted and "J's" mother and I did a little investigating. "J's" mother needed more validation. She clearly remembered "J" being hurt in that day care, thus the subsequent removal. But she wanted more proof. We were told that the day-care person had told "J's" mother that she was not licensed. After a bit more digging, we discovered that she was licensed. We also were told that, in fact, allegations had been brought against her in the past for suspected child abuse, neglect and willful misconduct. These charges had been "dropped." Further, we were told that in 1993 the day-care provider re-applied for licensure and was denied. However, she continued to "provide day-care."

The day-care provider is the "evil witch or monster." First as an externalized force of the actual abuser. Secondly, as "J" had internalized the experience and thereby formed a new and negative self-concept and manner of relating to her world.

Once the wounded part of herself, Two-tone is healed, she is free to celebrate and enjoy her new, positive identity. The story has a happy ending.

According to (Mills & Crowley, Therapeutic Metaphors for Children, etal, p.39), the importance of creating images in learning is crucial for children. "Hidden fears can be expressed, unspoken desires depicted, and problems acted out, all through fantasy."

The following is their list of functions of images in learning:

100

creation of (emotional) distance from the conflict

make things the way they like it/construction of an alternate reality

learn a different (and better) story of yourself

compatible with Erickson's "two-level" learning

(compensates for the contamination that he conflict creates)

it's fun and expresses the inner world of the child

makes sense of the world outside of self/the child can integrate

what is learned (into her behavior)

Moves on a healing journey toward what it looks like "all better."

STAGE FIVE OF PLAY (Norton's Experiential Model): TERMINATION STAGE: IT'S A WRAP!

Termination is an important stage of therapy for the child and the idea of it should be introduced after the child has experienced empowerment, relief from the symptoms they were suffering from, positive play in the playroom that reflects enjoyment and is developmentally appropriate.

Towards the end of Stage IV the clinician knows that the child is getting ready for the termination stage of therapy. The therapist says something like, "You know, we won't be playing together forever.... or for too much longer...." Pay attention to the child's response to this information. Most of the time, the timing is correct. If not, you will know by the anxiety your statement creates in the child. Whenever possible, I ask the child to decide how many more times they want to come back and play, in order to give them a feeling of control over their lives - but I limit the numbers from two to five. Sometimes this decision is a managed care or financial decision, so be aware of that before you give numbers for the child to pick. When the child says "100," smile and say: "I know you really like to play in here, but sometimes friends have to say good-bye."

Obviously, it is very important that the child does not feel rejected or abandoned by the Termination Stage of therapy. Expect a mild and short regression in a child's behavior during termination because the child will experience a brief feeling of her life being out of control again. I try to get the parents to arrange for some class or new learning situation for the child and put termination in the context of "graduation." I say, "I know you have played hard in here and you have been a great player! Now, you are graduating and you get to learn something new. I heard you will learn to be a karate guy or a dancing girl."

Put in this context of achievement coupled with new things, the child feels proud of graduating and leaving the playroom is a much easier transition.

Providing a transition for the child also puts the reason for termination into a context they can understand and hopefully, look forward to. It is very difficult to give up a relationship that has supported, empowered and accepted you no matter how you acted. Children need to know that leaving is a natural part of the whole process.

In this final and important stage, therapeutic responses go deep. Responses are based on the real quality of the relationship. Many responses are of a general nature but are focused on separation issues. Some self-disclosure is ok: "I am going to miss you but when I think about you, I'll think about you playing and being happy." The goal is to ensure and model a healthy separation of friends who need to say good by.

Use the play to say Good-bye to the toys, the play, the playroom and the therapist.

Parental Considerations: It is very important to have sufficient time to process termination with the child. Depending on the sophistication of the parent, they understand this. Three termination sessions are the minimum for 3-6 months of therapy. Longer treatment may require 5-6 closure sessions in order to ensure successful separation.

Some children may want to use EMDR to process feelings of separation and saying "goodbye." I give children a "good-bye" gift that will hopefully symbolize something important about our time together and the child's story.

EMDR is well utilized to help process potential feelings of loss of the relationship but use it *prior to the last session.* It seems best to just let the child play during their last session, again to ensure a feeling of control and to let the child say good-bye naturally.

Additionally, if requested by the parent, I will provide a "Termination or Therapeutic Summary," to parents as a part of their child's

"Keepsakes," because ultimately the power of good triumphs over the power of evil. The child who has been through this process knows that in their heart.

Because the use of EMDR has been fully established at this point of termination which is a very important component in the full completion of the "healing journey," children will ask to use EMDR to process feelings about saying good-bye. This is not as easy as using EMDR in the energized and positive stage of Therapeutic Growth but is nevertheless useful. It helps children to realize that it is ok to part, that the relationship has indeed been special and that you and the child will always be connected. Using the light technique to establish the heart to heart connection is a positive and healthy way to wrap it up!

REFERENCES

The Stories Children Tell, Making Sense of the Narratives of Childhood, Susan Engel, 1995, WH Freeman & Co.

Therapeutic Metaphors for Children and the Child Within, Dr. Joyce Mills & Dr. Richard J. Crowley, 1986, Brunner/Mazel, Inc.

Play Therapy, The Art of the Relationship, Garry L. Landreth, 1991, Accelerated

Development, Inc.

Eye Movement Desensitization & Reprocessing, Basic Principals, Protocols and Procedures, Francine Shapiro, 1995, The Guilford Press.

Therapeutic Stories for Children in Foster Care, Karen Landers and Ken Schwatenberger, Copyright 1992.

Play Therapy, (Revised ed.) Virginia Axline, 1969, New York, Ballentine Books.

The Healing Power of Play: Working with Abused Children, Eliana Gil, 1991, The Guilford Press.

Casualities of Childhood: A Developmental Perspective on Sexual Abuse Using Projective Drawings, Bobbie Kaufman and Agnes Whol, Brunner/Mazel, N.Y.

"The Erica Method," A Technique for Play Therapy and Diagnosis: A Training Guide, Margareta Sjolund, Ph.D.

EMDR: The Breakthrough Therapy for Overcoming Anxiety, Stress and Trauma,

Francine Shapiro, Ph.D and Margot Silk Forrest, 1997, Basic Books/a Division of HarperCollins, Pub., Inc.

Reaching Children Through Play Therapy: An Experiential Approach, Carol Crowell Norton, Ed.D and Byron E. Norton, Ed.D 1997, The Publishing Cooperative, Denver, CO.

Nursery Crimes: Sexual Abuse in Day Care, David Finkelhor, Linda Meyer Williams with Nanci Burns, 1988, SAGE Publications, Inc.

I

Using EMDR with Children, Ricky Greenwald, Psy.D, Copyright 1993.

Excerpts from Dr. Robert Tinker, Ph.D., CS., CO.

Annual Progress In Child Psychiatry &Child Development, 1996, Hertzog & Farber

Inside the Brain, Revolutionary Discoveries of How the Mind Works, Ronald Kotulak, Andrews McMeel Publishing, Kansas City, 1996.

A CHILDREN'S THERAPY PLACE, P.C.

SUPERVISION INFORMATION

Victoria McGuinness is the founding director of ACTP,PC. She has been in the field of therapy since 1983. Her credentials are as follows: M.A.L.P.C., EMDR II, CAC III (expired), RPT/S, CPT-S and is a nationally certified parent educator/trainer. Victoria's experience involves 18 years of working with women's issues, issues of sexual abuse in women and children, chemical dependency, play/sand therapy and EMDR with both adults, adolescents and children. Supervision often includes strategies for working with other agencies, parents, attorneys, the judicial system, etc. when involved with a child's case and ways to protect the therapeutic relationship in today's system.

Victoria provides supervision toward: LPC, and RPT or RPT/S. I do not provide EMDR supervision per se, but can supervise the use of integrating EMDR with play therapy. Supervision is available according to your needs. After a supervision agreement is arranged that both parties find mutually acceptable, supervision is available in person, by phone, through videos and by e-mail.

Supervision fee: $85.00 per session which is usually about one hour but sometimes is a bit longer or shorter depending on the case.

For more information please contact Victoria at: 719-386-0870 or by facsimile: 719-386-0872

Email: vicmcplay@akidstherapyplace.com

www.akidstherapyplace.com

A CHILDREN'S THERAPY PLACE P.C.

EARTHEART FOR KIDS, INC.

Phone: (719) 386-0870 FAX: (719) 386-0872

A GUIDE FOR PARENTS

WHAT IS PLAY THERAPY?

Playing is a child's work; children learn almost everything while playing. As experiential learners, play is a child's language and toys are the child's words. Play therapy is a special process that focuses on children's need to express themselves through the use of toys in play. Children are encouraged to play as they wish with a trained play therapist. Who provides a save and understanding environment for the young child in therapy. In this process, a wide variety of toys are made available to children to encourage the expression of emotional concerns. Children are given the opportunity to express themselves through a variety of styles including art, sand-tray, dramatic play and fantasy play.

WHY IS PLAY THERAPY BETTER FOR MY CHILD THAN OTHER FORMS OF THERAPY?

Playing is a natural force in children; children like to play. Children are generally not able to understand or verbally express their feelings or experiences the way adults do. This makes adult forms of treatment inappropriate in meeting the special needs of young children. Play becomes a therapeutic process to children as they give expression to their experiences and emotions. During play therapy sessions, children can recreate the experiences that are part of their anger, fear, sadness or frustration currently influencing their behavior. A special benefit of play therapy is that the child can crate therapeutic play at their own developmental level. The relationship with the therapist allows children a sense of security when recreating emotionally stressful experiences.

WHAT HAPPENS DURING THE PLAY THERAPY PROCESS?

Children are able to create play in the experiential play therapy process that resembles the emotional experiences they are struggling with internally. Children, in general, cannot verbalize these experiences; instead, they will select special toys to include in their play and use those toys to recreate issues that represent emotional conflicts that are important to the child and the healthy emotional development of the child. Beginning with this form of expression, the child's play evolves until the child gains a sense of understanding, mastery and comfort over a troubling situation.

HOW DOES PLAY THERAPY REALLY HELP MY CHILD?

When the child engages in the vivid and liberating "games" of play therapy, self-esteem increases which positively influences the child's relationships with others. Children and their parents can understand and enjoy each other more. This can happen because during the play therapy process, children can change their personal view of events in the world and begin to better enjoy their interactions with others. When children recreate their frustrations or disappointments and then change the experience of that situation in their play, they begin to enjoy more of their play experiences and therefore, more of life's interactions. This leads to higher self-esteem and more enjoyment of activities with family, friends and peers. It will certainly make parenting more enjoyable.

HOW LONG WILL MY CHILD BE IN THERAPY?

There are several factors involved in the answer to this question. One is that play therapy is a process that depends on several conditions in the child's past and present experiences. Two of the most important factors are the developmental stage of the child presently. The other is the age of the child at the onset of the issue. Generally speaking, the more recent the events, the shorter the length in therapy. The further back in the child's development that the onset of the issue occurred, the longer the play process will take.

HOW IS PLAYING IN THE PLAYROOM DIFFERENT THAN WHEN MY CHILD PLAYS AT HOME?

Play serves the same basic function in both situations because playing is a natural way for children to rehearse for life's interactions and demands. Play basically serves three purposes: 1). To facilitate cognitive development, 2). To facilitate motor development and 3). To facilitate emotional purposes. This leads to understanding and reestablishment of balance in the child's sense of well-being. Children discover new ways of coping which emerge in the special process of experiential play therapy.

HOW WILL I BE INVOLVED AS THE CHILD'S PARENT(S)?

Parent involvement is encouraged and supported by most TRAINED play therapists because parental involvement is very important to the play therapy process. Parents will consult on a regular basis with the therapist. A parent may become involved by joining in the play process, if recommended by the therapist and desired by the child. Parents are asked to contribute to their child's progress by following the recommendations of the therapist which may include activities outside of the play therapy room that supports the therapy process. Another important part parents play is to keep the therapist informed of any major changes in the child's life or emotional tone that need to be addressed in therapy.

USING EMDR AND PLAY THERAPY WITH YOUR CHILD

EMDR stands for "Eye Movement Desensitization and Reprocessing" and is a promising new process for healing the painful memories and behaviors or disturbances of trauma. Often, symptomatic and emotional recovery from trauma could take years in therapy to resolve; the use of EMDR processing can shorten the length of treatment. During the past ten to twelve years while EMDR was developing and expanding, it has been found effective for treating a wide range of people. Children benefit as well as adults, generally at a much quicker pace. Research indicates that positive therapeutic results with EMDR have been reported wit a variety of populations including: combat veterans, phobics, panic disorders, crime victims of violent assault, witnesses of domestic violence, grieving issues, loss, childhood trauma, PTSD, sexual assault, accident and burn victims, victims of sexual dysfunction, clients at all stages of chemical dependency and dissociative disorders.

EMDR processing is based on the fact that the two hemispheres of the brain process information in fundamentally two different ways. Although it is each hemisphere's job to process information and essentially cooperate with the other hemisphere to integrate information, trauma research indicates that trauma itself can hinder the bran's ability to correctly process information. EMDR enhances the brain's natural ability to do that. Although the original vehicle for processing was the use of eye movements to stimulate

The bi-lateral processing, we now know that the eye movements themselves are not necessary for processing information. Children under the age of 7 or 8 years have trouble with the eye movements. Children diagnosed with ADHD often cannot participate comfortably in EMDR processing using eye movements. A variety of methods are effectively woven into with the play therapy process to achieve positive results. Therapists use sounds, hand-taps, toys, puppets, pictures and the "thera-tapper," lights and other creative ways to achieve the same results with children who do not like or cannot perform the eye movements.

EMDR was discovered and developed by California psychologist Francine Shapiro over the last twelve years. EMDR is a neurological process and has been used in the treatment of trauma and anxiety in mild

to severe cases. The therapist guides the client, yourself or your child
engage in rapid eye-movements or bi-lateral , sequential hand-taps o
sounds while the client thinks of (initially) happy and safe things an
progresses to focusing on the painful memory or event. With children, thi
may occur through the use of projective devices such as toys, art &/o
memories of salient features that can be tolerated by the child. Integratin
play therapy with EMDR combines two very powerful therapy methods.

For many children and other clients who suffer, this bi-latera
processing somehow "metabolizes" the memory so it is no longer able t
haunt its victim with persistent reruns. But, just as your child needs you
support during the process of experiential play therapy, they will nee
your support while participating in EMDR. When children revisit/reliv
the original reason for their unwanted behaviors or beliefs, it can be ver
painful for them to work through the feelings associated with that behavio
or belief. They need your support to get to the other side of th
disturbance and gain mastery over their powerful feelings.

Children who have developed ongoing problems such as nightmares
bedwetting, fear, anger, anxiety, behavior problems, depression, unwante
thoughts, phobias, hyper-arousal and exaggerated startle response ca
benefit from the combination of EMDR and play therapy. Other traum
reactions may include: denial, guilt, sadness, confusion, sleeping or eating
disturbances, acting younger than their years, aggressive acting ou
behaviors, acting "like a baby," clinging, demanding extra attention, los
of previous skills, engaging in excessive "bad" behaviors that requir
punishment, excessive "good" behavior that replaces the usual level o
maturity and playfulness, etc. It is important to remember that children'
symptoms can also be very subtle and that children's reactions to trauma i
often delayed from six to eight weeks from the event. Children love to
engage in play therapy; sometimes a little nudging is needed to have them
participate in EMDR. Older children tend to really like the EMDR proces
and report having made considerable emotional gains by using it.

Younger children who get "stuck" in play therapy will often benefi
from "unsticking" by engaging in EMDR if only for a minute or two.

NOTE: (Please be aware that if as your child's therapist I feel EMDR
will help your child, every effort will be made to integrate EMDR with the
play therapy process. However, there are some children who refuse to

X

engage in EMDR in spite of the therapist's best efforts. Sometimes, having a parent demonstrate the process to the child with the therapist will encourage the child to participate.)

Reactions such as those listed above can have long term and severely damaging effects on the healthy development of children and can last a lifetime, if left untreated. For several years now, clinicians world-wide have successfully used EMDR with children who have been traumatized (such as Oklahoma City). Play therapy and EMDR enhance each other and combining these two powerful methods can make therapy more cost-effective by moving the process along as well as demonstrating that treatment works and produces the changes that parents are hoping for.

As with play therapy, it is essential that the therapist be trained in EMDR (as well as play therapy) before using either method with your child. Most trained clinicians will be pleased to share their methods of therapy with you in an on-going parent consultation time in order to benefit your child.

Many people are enthused about the great potential for healing with EMDR. Not only is it a revolutionizing therapy, it is also changing the way people deal with crisis. EMDR was used in Oklahoma City after the bombing for victims and caretakers in 1995, with Vietnam war vets, victims of rape, domestic violence, abuse, loss, automobile accidents or other accidents. It is helpful in the treatment of the anxiety and low self-esteem associated with ADHD or other physiologically based disorders.

Children, in general, heal much more quickly than adults especially with parental support. Many efforts have been made to modify the adult protocol for using EMDR to make its use accessible and effective with children. Therapists in the United States have brought this training to therapists in Rowanda to facilitate healing there with the children victimized in South Africa.

EMDR and play therapy are non-drug therapies. Occasionally, children will be referred for further evaluation or testing. Play therapy is a particularly accurate assessment tool for diagnosing children's disorders. EMDR can often help distinguish between symptoms that mimic ADHD but are actually the result of a trauma or wrong thinking. Neither EMDR nor play therapy will make a neurological diagnosis change but both will help the everyday hurts and challenges associated with neurologica disturbances.

Client safety is the main priority with both play therapy and EMDR EMDR can only be used after a good repor has been established with a client of any age. Work begins with the establishment of a "safe place" which can be real or imaginary or a combination of the two where a client feels totally safe, secure and comfortable. If no "safe place" can be found with a child, the play therapy process will continue uninterrupted until a "safe place" can be created and accepted by the child. With some children ONLY "safe place" is used in EMDR processing. For others, the bi-lateral stimulation can begin to heal nightmares, bad memories, etc. Sometimes only positive beliefs are "installed" into the child's psyche. Sometimes "safe place" can be used to anchor and ground a child who has had a particularly difficult play session. Combining EMDR and Play therapy provides a plethora of possibilites to help you or your child overcome life's difficulties.

COMMON PARENTAL RESPONSES TO TRAUMA

Guilt

Anxious &/or over-protective

Sleep disturbances

Withdrawal from the child

Inconsistency with discipline or expectations

Over-indulgence, letting the child "get away" with things

To over-compensate for the loss or trauma

Focusing on the trauma instead of the child

Maximizing or minimizing the effects of the trauma

PARENTS GUIDE FOR FAMILY PLAY THERAPY SESSIONS

EXPERIENTIAL MODEL

"THINGS ARE DIFFERENT IN HERE"

Because your child has requested your presence in the playroom or because I have decided that your participation in your child's session will benefit your child the most, please take the time to read through this guide so that your responses to your child's words and play will facilitate the healing process.

Children communicate verbally and non-verbally through metaphor and by association.

1. Regular rules DO NOT apply. The guidelines & limits are as follows:

A). We play in the playroom (we only leave to go to the bathroom.)

B). The toys live here. Sometimes, while testing for safety, a child will ask to take a toy home with them. Let me set the limit on requests for toys.

C). Follow the child's lead; try to NOT suggest games, ways of doing things and instead say: "In here, (in life) it's up to you what we play." (or what color to choose, etc.) This response helps to foster self-reliance and responsibility. It is a way of breaking unnecessary dependence and empowering your child to made decisions.

D). Unless your child is very young 2.5 years or less, do not label toys with their ordinary value - the goal is to not limit your child's imagination and to give them as much leeway as possible for self-expression. Instead, say something like: "What does that look like to you?" or "In here, that can be anything you want it to be."

E). Children are given a 10 minute and a 5 minute warning that our time for playing will be ending. Generally, in family sessions, we clean up the playroom together. However, if your child refuses to help - let me lead the way. This is not a time for a power struggle over who cleans up or to reinforce the rules from home.

F).   Please do not discuss family or other dynamics in the playroom with your child present. Please arrange a time for parent consultation away from your child's ears by phone or in person. In fact, the less said to me the better. Focus on your child with your eyes and your body language. (Try to face your child with your body.)

G).   If your child hits you or otherwise intrudes upon your personal space or integrity, please feel free to set your limit with your child. "I'm not for hitting, you can pretend the bop bag is me and hit that." Try to control any anger that you may feel and state your limit with as much neutrality and confidence as possible. Remember: experiential play therapy seeks to heal and change the motivation BEHIND THE UNWANTED BEHAVIORS. Focus on your child and NOT the unwanted behaviors. I will set the playroom limits, you set your own personal limits.

H).   Remember, experiential play therapy is not the time to teach children their colors, numbers, etc. If your child says the letter "H" is the letter "P" - so be it. If this is hard for you because you are concerned that they will not learn correctly say: "Hummm, I guess in here that letter can be the letter "P." or "It looks like the letter "P" to you."

I).   When and if we play a board game, your child is allowed to make his or her own rules up. I always remind your child that while they are playing at home or at a friends, etc. that they will need to follow the rules. But, "in here, you can make up your own rules." If your child then makes up rules that are confusing or unfair or something else that feels negative, then remember that they are trying to tell you something about their life experience through their play. (ie: life isn't fair, I don't stand a chance, the rules keep changing.)

Giving your child control of the game not only reveals their experience with a situation in life but reveals their defenses, need for control and ability to cope with reality.

Being in the playroom with your child provides some very effective ways to improve and heal your relationship with your child. There are a lot of things your child wants you to know about his or her life and his or her feelings. Some of these things will be difficult for you to accept, some will make you laugh, some will make you cry or feel angry or discouraged or encouraged. Please concentrate on accepting what your child is trying to tell you in each session even if it is difficult for you. Remember that it takes a lot of courage for your child to come to therapy and that they need your support. The rewards will come more quickly as you accept your child's feeling reality as valid and important. In so doing, you will see your relationship improve.

ABOUT THE AUTHOR

Victoria McGuinness is the founding director of A Children's Therapy Place, P.C. and EartHeart For Kids, Inc. In the field for over twenty years, Victoria has devoted herself to reaching and teaching people about the healing benefits for families utilizing experiential play therapy and ways to parent the "new kids." A Children's Therapy Place P.C. provides individual and family experiential play therapy to young children (ages two to twelve years) and their families as well as a variety of other developmentally appropriate therapies.

Victoria is a Registered Play Therapist and Supervisor both nationally and internationally. She holds certifications in EMDR, Parenting and formerly spent twelve years in the field of addictions. "Integrating Play Therapy and EMDR With Children" is a popular workshop. Victoria is currently writing a book on spirituality and parenting the "new kids." Please check: www.akidstherapyplace.com to preview the new book.

Please feel free to email Victoria @ vicmcplay@akidstherapyplace.com with any questions or comments, or to obtain play therapy supervision or training information.

CPSIA information can be obtained
at www.ICGtesting.com
Printed in the USA
FSOW02n0934221016
26454FS